P9-AQB-815

INDIANA LEARNS:

Increasing Indiana Student Academic Achievement Through School Library Media and Technology Programs

David V. Loertscher

with

Connie Champlin

Special Edition, AIME, November, 2002

WITHDRAWN

MONTGOMERY COUNTY PUBLIC SCHOOLS
PROFESSIONAL LIBRARY
850 HUNGERFORD DRIVE
ROCKVILLE, MARYLAND 20850

Hi Willow Research and Publishing

2002

NOV 15 2005

© 2002 Hi Willow Research and Publishing
All rights reserved.

Companion website for this book:

http://www.indianalearns.org

Copies of this publication are available through:
LMC Source
PO Box 131266
Spring TX 77393
800-873-3043 sales
936-271-4560 fax

Email: sales@lmcsource.com
Web page: http://www.lmcsource.com

Comments and suggestions to:
David V. Loertscher at davidl@wahoo.sjsu.edu

ISBN: 0-931510-85-6

(copies of up to 3 pages may be made for school or district inservice workshops as long as the source with ordering information is included in the reprints. All other copying is prohibited without the prior written permission of the publisher. Permission can be sought by e-mail at sales@ lmcsource.com)

ACKNOWLEDGEMENTS

Appreciation is extended to:

Dorothy Crenshaw
Director, Telecommunications and
Instructional Media, Indianapolis
Public Schools

Laura Taylor
Director, Office of Learning
Resources, Indiana Dept. of
Education

Judy R. Williams
Consultant, Office of Learning
Resources, Indiana Dept. of
Education

Marge Cox
Media Services Director,
Noblesville School District,
Noblesville, IN

Lorie Homan
Technology Specialist, Noblesville
School District, Noblesville, IN

Sue Cox
Consultant

Carolyn White
Consultant, Indiana Dept. of
Education

Michelle Bridgewater
Consultant, Indiana Dept. of
Education

Ken Scales
Director, Indiana Web Academy

About the Authors

David V. Loertscher is professor of library and information science at San Jose State University. He has been a library media specialist in Nevada and Idaho; has a Ph.D. form Indiana University, and has taught at Purdue University, The University of Arkansas, and The University of Oklahoma. He is a past president of AASL (American Association of School Librarians) and received their Distinguished Service Award in 2002.

Connie Champlin is a teacher, school library media specialist, author, and consultant. In Indiana, she has been the Coordinator of Media Services for the MSD of Washington Township and Director of Media Technology for the MSD of Pike Township.

CONTENTS

INTRODUCTION:

THE VISION OF LIBRARY MEDIA AND TECHNOLOGY PROGRAMS

The need to re-conceptualize school libraries has never been greater. The rush of technology has caused some to ask, "Is a school library media center needed?" "Is any library needed?" "Isn't it all on the Internet?" "Can't I just surf the Internet what I need?" Regular library and Internet users understand the benefits of integrating all forms of information technologies into a full-service organization with human interfaces as guides to the best and most practical information sources. In schools recently networked and upgraded for extensive technology use, the entire staff understands that the immense investment is only worthwhile if it translates into improved learning opportunities—and that key people make it happen!

In Indiana, Public Law 221 sets out a clearly definable set of expectations of what a quality education is for the children in the state. Both expectations and accountability provisions have been put in place to provide benchmarks along the path toward improvement. The library media and technology programs of the state have an enormous opportunity and responsibility to do their share to stimulate learning.

This volume is designed to help library media specialists and technology specialists take a leadership position in the state-wide initiative. It examines the type of program that will maximize learning for every child. Finally, it provides not just the vision for what should be happening, but it includes a plethora of ideas, plans, and resources to help make good things happen.

A companion volume to this one was created in 2000 entitled: *Reinventing Indiana School Libraries in the Age of Technology: A Guide for Superintendents and Principals.* That slim volume provided one-page ideas for rethinking the library media centers when administrators have little time to focus on so many administrative concerns. That same one-page, one-idea format has been preserved in this volume designed for the busy library media specialist and technology specialist.

 To extend this book beyond what is possible in a few pages, a web site has been established to provide access to a number of more in-depth publications and web-based resources. That site is organized by page number, matching the paging in this volume. Most pages have such extensions and resources will change over time. Users of this volume are encouraged to check that site at

http://www.indianalearns.org

The book is divided into six main sections that discuss:

> ➤ The **Introduction** to and vision of the library media and technology programs.
> ➤ **Data-driven practice**.

> **Collaboration** between teachers and library media specialists/technology specialists in the design of learning.
> Building avid and capable readers (**Reading**),
> Enhancing learning through **Technology**.
> Creating an information literate learner.(**Information Literacy**)

To further help the reader identify the content of the various pages, the page heading will indicate whether the page emphasizes
1. Vision,
2. Ideas and Resources, or
3. Assessment

Examples:
Reading — Vision
Technology — Assessment

Within each section, pages have been designed in such a way that each can be used as a handout for a workshop, an interview, a planning session. Many pages contain checklists to stimulate thinking and planning. Feedback to the authors is appreciated at [davidl@wahoo.sjsu.edu] or to the publisher.

Some important additional companion publications of value in amplifying this vision are:

	*Reinventing Indiana's Library Media Programs in the Age of Technology: A Handbook for Superintendents and Principals.* Hi Willow Research and Publishing, 2001. Designed as a quick guide to essential ideas about what constitutes a 21st century library media program and how to insure that schools have the elements, the staff, and the support needed to accomplish the goal of a high quality educational program.
	Loertscher, David V. *Taxonomies of the School Library Media Program.* 2nd ed. San Jose, CA: Hi Willow Research and Publishing, 2000. This book contains a comprehensive treatment of all the program elements of the school library media program and can be considered an extension of this *Reinvent* book.
	*NCREL's enGauge: 21st Century Skills: Digital Literacies for a Digital Age.* Naperville, IL: North Central Regional Educational Laboratory, 2002. A web-based framework that describes six essential conditions, or system wide factors critical to the effective use of technology for student learning. Survey instruments allowing districts and schools to conduct online assessments of system wide educational technology effectiveness are available on the enGauge website at: http://www.ncrel.org/engauge/
	*Eight Steps to Highly Effective 'Next Generation' Professional Development for Learning and Technology – Public Law 221 and Beyond.* Published in 2001 by the Indiana Department of Education, it can be used to created high-level professional development programs that will build a high-quality learning and teaching environment in every school. LMS/TS can not only benefit themselves from such developmental programs, but can also create quality professional development opportunities for their schools and districts.

Successful Learners in the 21ˢᵗ Century

"The driving force for the 21ˢᵗ century is the intellectual capital of citizens.[1]" When an exemplary library media and technology program is in place, every young person can be equipped with:

Reading Literacy ——→ 1. An Avid and Capable Reader.

Technology Literacy ——→ 2. A Skilled User of Technology Tools.
3. An Enhanced Learner.

Information Literacy ——→ 4. An Organized Investigator.
5. A Critical Thinker.
6. A Creative Thinker.
7. An Effective Communicator.
8. A Responsible Information User

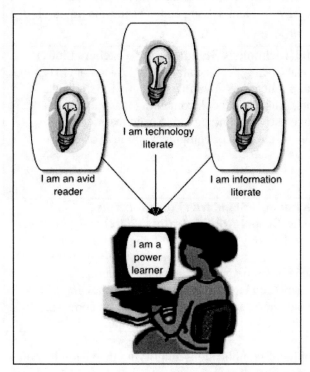

Learners who thrive in quality library media and technology programs become power learners because they are equiped with powerful learning tools. Combined with what they know and are able to perform or do, learners are prepared to thrive in the 21st century.

---

[1] *NCREL's enGuage: 21ˢᵗ Century Skills: Digital Literacies for a Digital Age,* Naperville, IL: North Central Regional Educational Laboratory, 2002. p. v.

National Standards and Guidelines

There are two nationally published documents by AASL and ISTE that can offer invaluable guidance in creating library media programs and technology initiatives in the school. Both associations make information available to teachers on a wide variety of issues related to libraries and technology. Are these documents available in your school? Are they used?

	**Information Power: Building Partnerships for Learning (1998)** These national guidelines are a joint publication of the American Association of School Librarians (AASL) and The Association for Educational Communications and Technology (AECT) published in 1998. The book not only describes a progressive and dynamic school library media program, but provides nine major standards for information literacy - the ability to find and use information – as a keystone of lifelong learning.
	**National Education Technology Standards for Students (2001)** NETS (National Educational Technology Standards) provides performance indicators of what students should know about and be able to do with technology by the completion of Grades 2, 5, 8, and 12. Six broad categories are addressed: basic operation and concepts; social, ethical, and human issues; technology productivity tools; technology communication tools; technology research tools; and technology problem solving and decision-making tools.
	**National Educational Technology Standards for Teachers (2001)** Prepared by the International Society for Technology in Education (ISTE) in 2000, this is one of several publications covering standards for students, teachers and administrators, plus a handbook containing many examples of instructional units that make use of technology to expand learning. These standards go far beyond the installation of equipment and networks.
	Making Technology Standards Work for You – A Guide for School Administrators (2002) Offers administrators and technology leaders a step-by-step approach to develop and implement a vision for using educational technology more effectively. Chapters include planning, curriculum and instruction, assessment, staff development, and legal and social issues—showing how to assess what is in place already and determine what needs to be done next. It includes the "Technology Standards for School Administrators (TSSA).

Note: Both ISTE and AASL have a variety of helpful publications amplifying the vision in their standards documents. Check their web pages for a list of resources:

ISTE: http://www.iste.org

AASL: http://www.ala.org/aasl/index.html

Making Sense of Public Law 221

The Indiana General Assembly passed Public Law 221[1] in 1999 that governs school improvement and accountability. The following aims of education represent the combined vision of policymakers, educators, parents, students, business and community leaders for education in Indiana:

Indiana's Aims for Education

(Aims describe the purpose of an organization, in this case the educational opportunities to be provided students in Indiana schools. Goals are products – educational programs, services, and resources – required to meet the aims and for which we will hold ourselves accountable. Goals therefore, must be measurable.)

Indiana will provide:

1. Safe and caring schools.
2. High standards, assessments, and accountability.
3. High-performing system preparing high-performing, responsible, and responsive citizens.
4. High student achievement.
5. Effective use of resources.

Source: http://www.doe.state.in.us/asap/aimsgoals.html

The Indiana state aims have been translated into academic standards documents designed to guide schools in curriculum development. Local schools are to *align* their curriculum with the state aims using ISTEP+ assessments of student learning and accreditation of a school as a signpost of continuous school improvement. This process is illustrated below:

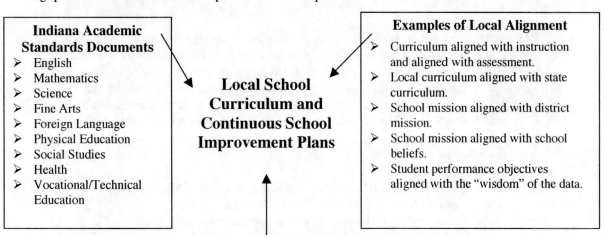

Indiana Academic Standards Documents
- English
- Mathematics
- Science
- Fine Arts
- Foreign Language
- Physical Education
- Social Studies
- Health
- Vocational/Technical Education

Local School Curriculum and Continuous School Improvement Plans

Examples of Local Alignment
- Curriculum aligned with instruction and aligned with assessment.
- Local curriculum aligned with state curriculum.
- School mission aligned with district mission.
- School mission aligned with school beliefs.
- Student performance objectives aligned with the "wisdom" of the data.

Assessment Data Sources for School Improvement Tracking
- ISTEP+
- Accreditation

---

[1] Much valuable information concerning the law and its implementation over time are available on the state website at: www.doe.state.in.us/pl221 and at www.doe.state.in.us/asap

Information Literacy and Technology Literacy in Indiana Standards

Information and technology literacy standards are embedded in the Indiana academic standards. Indiana does not have separate information literacy or technology literacy standards. Technology is seen as a tool to help students achieve the academic standards. The expectation is that technology will be used as appropriate to teach the academic standards. In the Curriculum Frameworks, model lesson plans for each standard at each grade level, suggestions are included for how technology supports the standard/lesson. Sample statements from standards documents are given below.

In this technological age, mathematics is more important than ever. When students leave school, they are more and more likely to use mathematics in their work and everyday lives---operating computer equipment, planning timelines and schedules, reading and interpreting data, comparing prices, managing personal finances, and completing other problem-solving tasks. What they learn in mathematics and how they learn it will provide an excellent preparation for a challenging and ever-changing future.

The Indiana Council of Teachers of Mathematics (ICTM) and the Indiana Mathematics Initiative (IMI) recommend use of NCTM principles and standards to Indiana teachers as a basis for effective implementation of Indiana's Math Standards. The technology principle in the NCTM Standards states that technology is essential in teaching and learning mathematics; it influences the mathematics that is taught and enhances students learning. That principle further states, "Students can learn more mathematics more deeply with the appropriate and responsible use of technology."

Standard 4, Writing Process, of English/Language Arts includes Research and Technology, which requires students to develop presentations based on a variety of print and electronic sources and to use technology for all aspects of creating, revising, editing, and publishing. Standard 7, Listening and Speaking, asks students to analyze oral and media communications and to deliver multimedia presentations that demonstrate a comprehensive understanding of literary works and support important ideas and viewpoints through references to the text and other works.

The first Science standard focuses on the nature of science and technology. This first standard draws portraits of science and technology that emphasize their roles in scientific endeavor and reveal some of the similarities and connections between them.

Resource: See all the state standards and resources to support them at http://doe.state.in.us/standards/welcome.html

The Changing Library Media Center

Twice in this century, school libraries have undergone a major redesign. The first was in the 1960s when book libraries had to be rethought to include a new wave of audiovisual devices and software. The second began in the 1980s with the proliferation of the microcomputer, computer networks and the Internet. The first redesign required only a shift in contents. The second requires an entire rethinking.

We have usually thought of the library as the "hub of the school," a place where everyone comes to get materials and equipment. Now, however, in the age of technology, the library media center becomes "Network Central" with its tentacles reaching from a single nucleus into every space of the school and into the home. Where we once thought of the library as a single learning laboratory, now the entire school becomes a learning laboratory served by the LMC/Technology Center. It becomes both centralized and decentralized at the same time.

OLDER LIBRARY CONCEPT   NEWER LMC/TECHNOLOGY CONCEPT

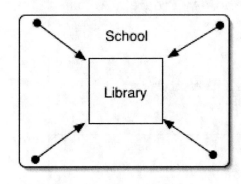
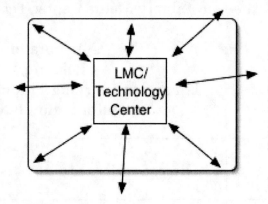

Older	**Newer**
Print rich	Information rich in every format
Print and AV oriented	Multiple technologies
Centralized (one location)	Centralized / decentralized simultaneously
Rigidly scheduled	Flexibly scheduled
Single person staff	Professional, technical, and support staff
A quiet, almost-empty place	A busy, bustling learning laboratory
Open during school hours	Online services 24 hours a day, seven days a week.

With the advent of high technology and sophisticated networks, many schools have approached high technology as if it were separate and distinct from "the library." But after the networks are in and the equipment in place, it soon becomes evident that materials and information merely have new paths to take. The concept of a vast store of materials and information poised to serve teachers and learners remains intact no matter what it is named — the library, the library media center, or the information technology center.

The Library Media Center/Technology Program as a Focal Point to Achieve Learner Success

To stimulate all learners to reach their potential in the information world, the library media center staff and technology staff concentrate on four major program areas sitting atop the school information infrastructure. These four central program elements are the foundation of increased academic achievement. The entire library media center and technology staff concentrate on the program elements to build the desired impact.

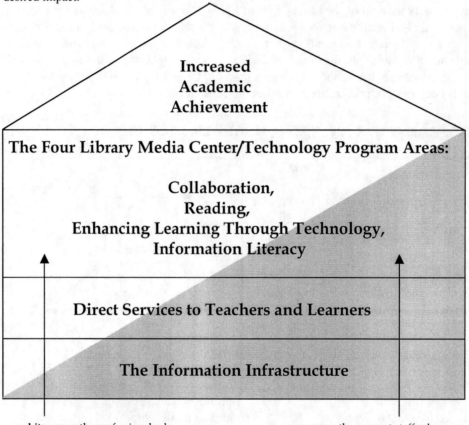

Increased
Academic
Achievement

The Four Library Media Center/Technology Program Areas:

Collaboration,
Reading,
Enhancing Learning Through Technology,
Information Literacy

Direct Services to Teachers and Learners

The Information Infrastructure

white area = the professional role   **gray area** = the support staff role

➤ **The Information Infrastructure** in the library media center/tech facility provides the technological foundation for delivering materials and information in all media formats. It is composed of the networking, the equipment, staffing, budget, facilities, repair and technical support for every kind of technology including print, multimedia, video, and digital.

➤ **Direct Services to Teachers and Learners** provides personalized services — the human interface.

➤ **The Library Media Center/Technology Program** is a tool for using all the technologies in such a way that teaching and learning are affected in major positive ways.

➤ **Increased Academic Achievement** is the outcome. In addition to academic achievement as a central thrust, there are a host of other personal benefits to a student and teacher who use technology and information well, such as becoming a lifelong reader, an independent learner, successful seeker of information, and a career builder, among others.

School Library Media Programs and Achievement: What the Research Says:

Ten Major Studies done since 1993 in over 3,300 schools:

Indiana	Alaska
Pennsylvania	Colorado (2 studies)
Texas	Oregon
Iowa	New Mexico
Massachusetts	Scotland

Strong school library media programs make a difference in academic achievement. This happens when the library media center has a high quality information-rich and technology-rich environment, easily accessible to students and teachers, and when there is both professional and support personnel who provide leadership and tireless partnering. Significant contributions happen in spite of the presence of at-risk factors.

The findings are quite consistent across the various states. The bottom line seems to be that a good school library media program collaborating with a teacher will transform information technology into quality learning experiences thus affecting achievement even when at-risk factors are present as pictured below:

Sources

➢ Web site for this book http://www.indianalearns. org

➢ http://lrs.org - Colorado Dept. of Ed. Tracks these studies.

➢ Lance, Keith and David V. Loertscher. *Powering Achievement*. 2nd edition. Hi Willow Research & Publishing, 2003.

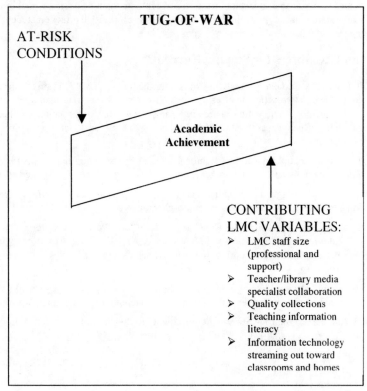

TUG-OF-WAR

AT-RISK CONDITIONS

Academic Achievement

CONTRIBUTING LMC VARIABLES:
➢ LMC staff size (professional and support)
➢ Teacher/library media specialist collaboration
➢ Quality collections
➢ Teaching information literacy
➢ Information technology streaming out toward classrooms and homes

Does Technology Enhance Learning?
What the Research Says

Billons have been spent equipping schools nationwide with technology. Some felt that hooking in and logging on would be a panacea for the nation's educational problems, when in reality, a long-term innovation was being introduced akin to replacing horses with automobiles.

Expected Benefits of Technology for Learners

➤ Affecting what they know.
  o Enhancing their ability to grasp and retain concepts
  o Enlarging their knowledge base
➤ Affecting what they can do.
  o Building their efficiency
  o Enhancing their information literacy
  o Enhancing their productivity
  o Building their skills for the world of work.
  o Connecting them to a quality information-rich environment at the elbow
➤ Affecting their attitude.
  o Engaging them as learners

Expected Benefits of Technology for Teachers

➤ Affecting what they teach
  o Enhancing the sophistication and amount taught
  o Enabling the teaching of a full range of state standards
➤ Affecting how they teach
  o Enhancing the ability to reach every learner
  o Assisting in management of classroom operations
  o Diversifying role, location, and time
➤ Affecting their expectations of learners
  o Expecting learners to learn more in less time
  o Responding to higher student engagement

And the Research Says:

"Technology is a means, not an end; it is a tool for achieving instructional goals, not a goal in itself."[1] "There is a substantial body of research that suggests that technology can have a positive effect on student achievement under certain circumstances and when used for certain purposes."[2]

Must Reads and Resources for Staying Current:

➤ CARET Funded by the Gates Foundation and under the umbrella of ISTE, this project bridges education technology research to practice by offering research-based answers to critical questions. Most importantly, users can connect to an automatic research reporting service that keeps the reader abreast of new studies dealing with the effectiveness of educational technology. Also check out their "helpful links" page. At: http://caret.iste.org/

➤ NCRTEC (North Central Educational Regional Laboratory) provides many tools for professional development, planning and evaluation, teaching and learning. At: http://www.ncrtec.org/

➤ enGague A website designed to help districts and schools plan and evaluate the system wide use of educational technology. At: http://www.ncrel.org/engauge/ec

➤ Kelley, Loretta and Cathy Ringstaff. *The Learning Return on Our Educational Technology Investment: A Review of Findings from Research*. San Francisco, CA: WestEd, 2002. At: http://www.wested.org/cs/wew/view/rs/619 - presents a current overview of selected major studies in the use of computer technology for learning.

➤ "SRI Technology Design Meeting Web Site" at http://www.sri.com/policy/designkt/found.html provides numerous recent studies in full text concerning the impact of technology on education.

➤ "Using Computers to Improve Student Achievement" Essay and link to research studies done at NCREL. At: http://www.ncrel.org/sdrs/areas/issues/methods/technlgy/te800.htm

---

[1] Kelley, Loretta and Cathy Ringstaff. *The Learning Return on Our Educational Technology Investment: A Review of Findings from Research*. San Francisco, CA: WestEd, 2002, p. 1.
[2] *Ibid.*, p. 24

Library Media Specialists and Technology Specialists
Shared and Collaborative Roles

Depending on local circumstances and organizational structure, two professionals and their supporting staff have a vital stake in insuring that both information and high technology contribute to learning. The staffing pattern in various school corporations is evolving as the library media program and the technology program collaborate and meld into a cohesive information technology environment. In some schools, there are both library media and technology specialists. In other buildings there is a single professional with clerical and technical staff. The resulting program will require a set of functional elements to be able to stimulate learning and teaching.

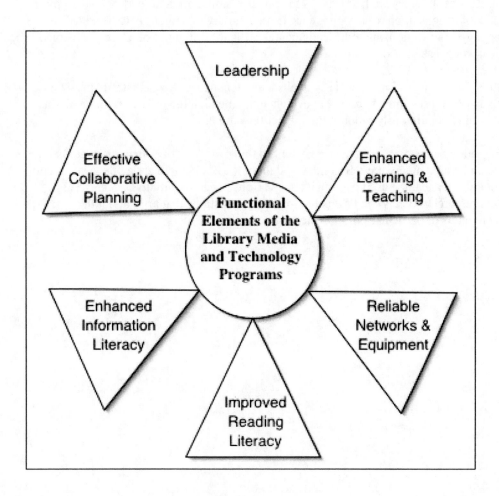

Data-Driven Practice

Data-Driven Practice

Educators at all levels are being asked to collect various forms of evidence about the impact of actions upon results. Evidence from a variety of sources is to be added to experience, perception, and other judgmental skills to form more objective decisions. This is known as data-driven practice.

Within this section, library media specialists and technology specialists are presented with an overall scheme of collecting evidence upon which the program can be measured and used to continuously monitor the impact they are having.

The section begins with the encouragement to think in terms of collecting ongoing data that can be used at any time. Second, throughout the book, there are evidence collection techniques that can be used periodically as various program initiatives occur. Third, action research projects can be created to answer questions that arise about the effectiveness of particular program elements.

Backwards Planning

"To begin with the end in mind means to start with a clear understanding of your destination. It means to know where you are going so that you better understand where you are now so that the steps you take are always in the right direction." (Stephen R. Covey: *The Seven Habits of Highly Effective People*. New York: Simon & Schuster, 1989.)

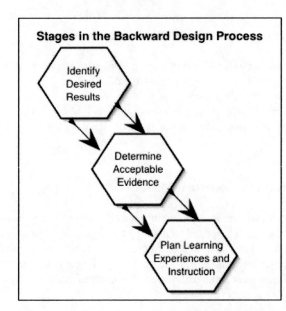

Stages in the Backward Design Process

Identify Desired Results

Determine Acceptable Evidence

Plan Learning Experiences and Instruction

The backward design process is a strategy advocated by Grant Wiggins and Jay McTighe for creating learning experiences.[1] Rather than following the planning model of: set goals, create instructional activities, and assess the results, the two professionals begin at the end – that is, begin with the result, set up evidence of success, and then plan the activities to get there.

Such a model works well in Indiana because Public Law 221 and the various state standards documents set out the desired results for every learner and provide the ISTEP+ tests as one acceptable measure to use as evidence. To the adults guiding learning, the message is clear: there are a number of ways to achieve the targets and to measure the results, but the state expects the standards and the one prescribed measure to happen.

For example, we could say to learners: "Beginning in Fort Wayne and using ground transportation, travel to Evansville. Report your mileage using an odometer." The result and the measurement are clear: the routes can be varied.

If library media specialists and technology leaders are prepared to work with backwards planning and feel at ease with this technique, operating in a data-driven environment becomes a natural part of instructional planning. Since evidence is expected, professionals can build in data collection tools as a normal part of the everyday routine.

---

[1] Wiggins, Grant and Jay McTighe. *Understanding by Design*. Alexandria VA: ASCD, 1998, p. 9

Three Data-Driven Decision Making Strategies

As a part of the total school's data-driven decision making, the library media center and technology programs need to contribute their part to ongoing data to assess their impact on student achievement. This can be done using:

➤ Ongoing data collection instruments (daily, weekly, monthly measures).
➤ Data from the ongoing data collection to prepare reports or presentations.
➤ Action research projects (studies within the school or district designed to answer local questions).

Build Ongoing Data Collection Sets and Reporting Procedures

Set in motion various data gathering mechanisms that will monitor operations, program elements, and organizational support for regular analysis and reporting. They can be collected:

➤ In real time (for example, hits on an online database)
➤ Periodically (recording collaborations in a log book or database at the end of the day)
➤ For special projects (a time analysis of various activities on three typical days for a research project)

Data-driven Practices at Opportune Moments

There are numerous techniques that allow the professional staff to measure the effectiveness of various program elements as they occur. For example, the use of a special technology to make a new learning experience possible, or student use of online resources as cited in student products, or documenting the amount of learning and success of information literacy strategies in a learning experience. In isolation, a measure may not be impressive, but added to others over time, patterns emerge that provide evidence of impact.

Design Action Research Projects

A more formal approach to data-driven decision making is to conduct actual research projects that address specific questions about the effectiveness of the LMC and technology programs. A school-wide initiative or a grant may require documentation of impact. What we teach learners to do every day can be transformed into action research project design. Note the similarity between a generic information literacy model and an action research project design.

GENERIC INFORMATION LITERACY MODEL	ACTION RESEARCH PROJECT DESIGN
Build a Question	Build a research question; Create a methodology
Find and sort information	Collect data
Consume and absorb the information	Analyze the data
Think and create	Analyze, analyze, analyze
Summarize and conclude	Draw conclusions
Communicate	Report the results
Reflect on process and product	Reflect; Take action

Challenge: Design and carry out a mix of all three strategies as a part of contributing to the entire school's effort to carry out PL221.

Triangulation of Data-Driven Practice

Triangulation of data means to collect data from various points of view or vantage points before making a decision. To understand what an elephant is, better to get a view from the front, the rear and from the side rather than any single picture. Like the points of a triangle, there ARE different vantage points from which the impact on learning (the center of the triangle) can be

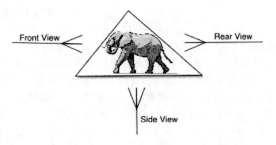

viewed or validated. The trend in state and federal governments is to ask educators to collect more quantitative (or scientific) data by using more rigorous research designs. Those designs often require experimental conditions difficult to create in local schools. To compensate, since learning and teaching are not exact sciences, the more types of data we collect, the closer our views of the elephant will move toward validity. At the same time, local communities will need to learn to accept a wide variety of indicators of success rather than exclusively seeking test score evidence.

Both library media specialists and technology specialists need to collect various evidences as a part of their effort to document what they contribute, what they do, and what they need to do next. Three major types of evidence suggested here, could be collected in any school to provide a more holistic view of the library media and technology programs:

Data from the organizational perspective. Common measures at the organization level are size of facilities, the equipment available, the amount of funding provided, and the size of collections or staff. All these factors might be termed "inputs" or the resources we have to make a difference. They are often reported to accrediting agencies and in local reports to administrators and boards. The Lance studies of LMC impact looked at many inputs as they affect the "output" – reading scores.[1]

Data from the learning unit level. Data can be collected about the various learning experiences that are designed by adults to interact with LMC materials and technology. That is, we begin examining the impact of our resources on teaching and learning. "Because we have this, we did that." Data collected from the collaborative activities of teachers and LMC staff are quite powerful in describing impact. For example, the Lance studies did note that achievement was affected as the amount of collaboration between teacher and LMS staff increased.[2]

Data from the learner level. Data at the learner level such as achievement test scores are currently at center stage in the United States. The ISTEP scores in Indiana have taken on great significance. There are, however, many other measures of how well an individual might be doing: portfolios, attitude, measures of performance, and other techniques used by both adults and learners to judge individual attainment.

The Challenge: To use measures from all levels to triangulate the view of impact.

---

[1] See Lance, Keith Curry and David V. Loertscher. *Powering Achievement*. 2nd edition. Hi Willow Research & Publishing, 2003.
[2] *Ibid*.

Learner Level
Data-Driven Practice
Triangulation of Data

During collaboration activities where teachers, library media specialists and technology specialists combine expertise to enhance a learning experience, all members of the collaborative team should be interested in and help create measures whereby a learner will know how successfully they are growing and developing as learners. The measures here are designed from the learner's point of view.

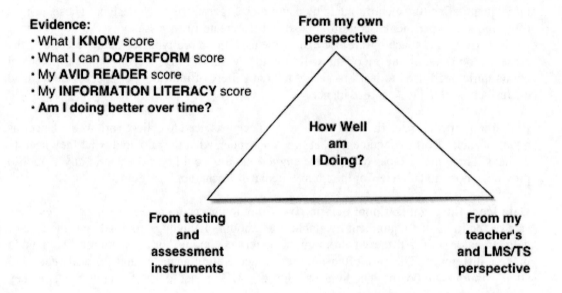

Evidence:
- What I **KNOW** score
- What I can **DO/PERFORM** score
- My **AVID READER** score
- My **INFORMATION LITERACY** score
- **Am I doing better over time?**

From my own perspective

How Well
am
I Doing?

From testing and assessment instruments

From my teacher's and LMS/TS perspective

FROM THE LEARNER PERSPECTIVE	TESTING AND ASSESSMENT	TEACHER, LMS, TS PERSPECTIVE
Grade point averages	State tests	Checklists/questionnaires
Self-scored rubrics	Local tests	Conferencing
Journals	Performance tests	Demonstrations / showcase / re-enactment
Checklists/questionnaires		Journals
My own avid reader score		Portfolios
My information literacy score		Project assessments
Self-assessment of progress		Rubrics

For more resources on assessment, see the web page for this book at http://www.indianalearns.org and http://ideanet.doe.state.in.us/technology

Learning Unit Level
Data-Driven Practice
Triangulation of Data

Probing the impact of the instructional program, when the LMC and technology are integral, allows three major measurements to take place. These are measurements from collaboration logs, rubrics, and assessments of learning. What learning experiences have been created to help students achieve? Has collaboration between the teacher and the LMC/TS staff affected the teacher's methods? How well have all the systems worked in support of the teacher? Did the impact of the LMC and technology program show up as a factor across learners in a classroom? In learner rubrics? In other assessment measures?

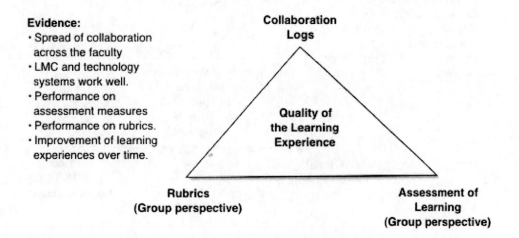

Evidence:
- Spread of collaboration across the faculty
- LMC and technology systems work well.
- Performance on assessment measures
- Performance on rubrics.
- Improvement of learning experiences over time.

Collaboration Logs

Quality of the Learning Experience

Rubrics (Group perspective)

Assessment of Learning (Group perspective)

Sources of evidence:

COLLABORATION MEASURES	RUBRICS (Group perspective)	ASSESSMENT OF LEARNING (Group Perspective)
Collaboration Logs	Quality of learning experience	Content learning
Impact!*	Contribution of technology	Product assessment
Collaborative units linked to LMC web page	Contribution of information literacy	Process assessment
Performance of LMC and technology systems		

*Miller, Nancy. Impact! (LMC Data Collection Analysis). San Jose, CA: Hi Willow, 2003.

For more resources on assessment, see the web page for this book at http://www.indianalearns.org and http://ideanet.doe.state.in.us/technology

Organization Level
Data-Driven Practice
Triangulation of Data

Professionals need to keep the school community apprized of the LMC and technology program performance at any given time and across the years. Organizational data including inputs, formal assessments, and staffing have been commonly collected over the years as professionals try to gauge whether there is a powerful learning environment for all learners.

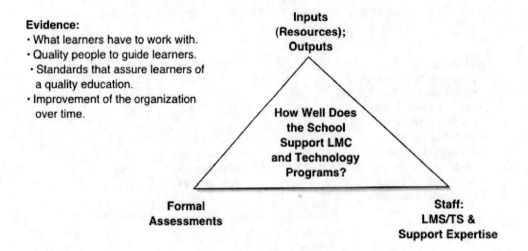

Evidence:
- What learners have to work with.
- Quality people to guide learners.
- Standards that assure learners of a quality education.
- Improvement of the organization over time.

Inputs (Resources); Outputs

How Well Does the School Support LMC and Technology Programs?

Formal Assessments

Staff: LMS/TS & Support Expertise

Sources of data:

INPUTS / OUTPUTS		FORMAL ASSESSMENTS	STAFF: LMS/TS & SUPPORT
Facilities	Use	Performance-based accreditation documents	Size and roles (professional & support)
Staffing	What they do	School improvement efforts	Certification; Endorsements
Collections	Use	District-level initiatives	LMS/TS National Board Certification (NBPTS)
Budgets	Collections; Databases	School library and technology audits	Personal growth plans
Administrative support	Program implementation		School-based performance evaluations
Technology infrastructure	Network use; Reliability		Growth in expertise over time (CE, professional organizations)

For more resources on assessment, see the web page for this book at http://www.indianalearns.org and http://ideanet.doe.state.in.us/technology

Examples of Data-Driven Practice Projects

Data-driven practice requires strategies to monitor how well programs put in place are operating. Below are several examples where data are collected at the learner, unit, and organizational levels.

Action	Learner-level Evidence	Unit-level Evidence	Organizational-level Evidence
LMS added Information literacy items to class project rubric.	Learners score themselves; LMS scores each student on info-lit. items; teacher uses total score.	LMS and teacher compare progress of class with previous unit experience.	Experience logged as part of policy shift to teach info lit on a "just-in-time" basis.
Teachers and LMS establish a book-bag program with K-2 learners; Each learner to read two books per night.	Learner and parent track amount read. Mini reading tests every month result in a reading progress chart.	Class progress charted and compared against expected gains; ISTEP reading scores monitored.	Skyrocketing use of books documented. A supplemental budget is provided to build the program.
Six high school AP chemistry students are taking a course by distance learning with other seniors across Indiana.	Local teacher coach has student report personal progress regularly monitoring attitude, assessments, and interaction with fellow students.	Teacher of record monitors group progress noting comparative progress and completion rates as compared with other DL courses.	Data on all student progress and completion rates via DL technology. TS provides evidence of technology system reliability.
LMS/TS work with 7th grade science teachers to plan semester units during a week-long summer institute.	Assessments of student learning planned to track individuals with the goal of 100% mastery of state science standards for the semester.	Group performances will be compared against previous two classes when teachers worked without involvement of LMS/TS.	Tracking of collaborative activities into a previously unserved curricular area is noted and reported.
After installation of a LMC home page connected to Inspire, the LMS/TS decide to compare users in classrooms that have the LMC page as default vs. those classrooms where the LMC home page is one or two clicks down.	Data clicks are measured by terminal rather than by individual students within each classroom.	Data clicks are combined for each classroom and compared across classrooms.	Decisions are made about the position the LMC homepage will have on computers in the classrooms. Results are compared across schools in the district that have similar technology.

Assessment Resources

Numerous techniques have been developed to assist in measuring the impact of educational programs and initiatives on learners and learning communities. The variety spans various sophistication levels and research methodologies. The emphasis in recent years has been toward more objective and scientific methodologies. However, human factors and ethical considerations do not allow us to treat learners as laboratory animals in our quest for predictive strategies that work. On this page, a few helpful resources for the more serious researcher are listed.

➢ Data in a Day (DIAD) is a 24-hour process through which a school can involve their entire community in a self-study. It is flexible and can be adapted for many purposes; it focuses on teaching and learning in the classroom, relies heavily on student voice, and has the potential to involve the entire school community. A complete description can be found in *Look Who 's Talking Now: Student Views of Learning in Restructuring Schools*. (Kushman, 1997) Also at: http://www.ael.org/rel/quest/dataday.htm

➢ Sagor, Richard. *Guiding School Improvement with Action Research*. Alexandria VA: ASCD, 2000. A guide to building local research studies for higher reliability and to feed sound decision-making.

➢ *Analysis of Process* – a technique of rating the conditions needed to enhance the organization's impact on teaching and learning. Created by Jim Cox, this technique and instrumentation is available through the Technology Information Center for Administrative Leadership (TICAL) at: http://www.portical.org/d3mtools.html (see "Identifying program elements to improve student achievement" under the Data Driven Decision-Making Tools)

➢ Porter, Bernajean. *Evaluating Student Computer-based Products: Training and Resource Tools for Using Student Scoring Guides*. Sedalia, CO: Bernajean Porter Consulting, 2001 – Provides extensive assistance in developing thorough rubrics to rate the learning contained in student products.

➢ **ICAN:** Individualized Curriculum and Assessment Notebook. Indiana Department of Education. At: http://www.ICANtech.com - a web-based software system that manages individualized curriculum, assessment, and analysis through standards-based accountability. Teachers use an elaborate computer program that helps them track what standards they are working on, track progress, and provides a reporting mechanism for analysis and for personal assessment of teaching.

The Quality of the Total Assessment
A Reflection

If data-driven practice is going to succeed, the various data-collecting mechanisms must work, but most importantly, not interfere with the LMC and technology programs. Professionals and support staff need not spend an inordinate amount of time trying to measure what is happening lest the act of measurement destroy the program itself. The following chart may assist the professional in designing and carrying out measurements that work.

Ongoing Data Collection

➢ Does it integrate easily into daily routines?	Yes	❑	❑	No
➢ Does it take little time/attention to gather?	Yes	❑	❑	No
➢ Is it immediately useful in pursuit of				
➢ school goals?	Yes	❑	❑	No
➢ Does it reflect accurately what really goes on?	Yes	❑	❑	No
➢ Is it easily analyzed and reported?	Yes	❑	❑	No
➢ Is it simple?	Yes	❑	❑	No

Action Research Project

➢ Is the research question clear?	Yes	❑	❑	No
➢ Is the research design sound?	Yes	❑	❑	No
➢ Are the data collection instruments well designed?	Yes	❑	❑	No
➢ Is the data collected accurate?	Yes	❑	❑	No
➢ Are statistical analyses properly used?	Yes	❑	❑	No
➢ Is the interpretation of the data thoughtful?	Yes	❑	❑	No
➢ Is the presentation of the results understandable?	Yes	❑	❑	No
➢ Are learning strategies changed based on the findings?	Yes	❑	❑	No

Collaborative Planning in the School Community for Library Media Centers and Technology Programs

Collaboration

Collaborative planning is defined as the teaming of teachers, library media specialists, and technology specialists to create exciting learning experiences that take advantage of the information-rich and technology-rich environment of the school.

No other concept of the role of the library media center program is more central or more vital to its success. Research of library media programs[1] draws the conclusion that collaborative planning is a strong link to achievement of learners. Collaborative planning turns the library media program and technology program from passive to active school initiatives. Judging by the amount of money required to build and maintain viable LMC and technology programs, a passive program is simply unacceptable. There are too many voices requesting funding to support any program not carrying its weight in meeting the requirements of PL 221.

Professionals who collaborate to build rich learning experiences find great satisfaction in knowing they make a difference. Their jobs are exciting, extremely busy, rewarding, and empowering. These professionals are recognized by their peers as being on the leadership team.

The first section of this book concentrates on the collaborative process of the teacher and the library media and technology specialists to plan, implement, and evaluate improved learning experience that will result in more learning.

---

[1] Lance, Keith and David V. Loertscher. *Powering Achievement*. 2nd ed. San Jose, CA: Hi Willow Research & Publishing, 2002.

Collaboration of Teachers/Library Media Specialists and Technology Specialists: What Is It?

As partners, the teacher, the library media specialist, and technology specialist, team to use materials, information, and information technology to enhance a learning activity.

Together, they:

Plan goals and objectives of the unit based on Indiana standards.

Complete preparations for the unit.

Jointly teach the learning activities.

Utilize technology to achieve learning objectives.

Integrate an information literacy skill as needed.

Assess learning and the learning process.

Assess the materials, information, and information technology used.

Such collaborative learning experiences can be a few days in length, several weeks, a semester, or even a yearlong project. The teacher might be a single person or a small group of teachers from several disciplines, a subject department, a grade-level team, or the faculty as a whole. Other specialists and the students themselves may be participants in the collaborative process.

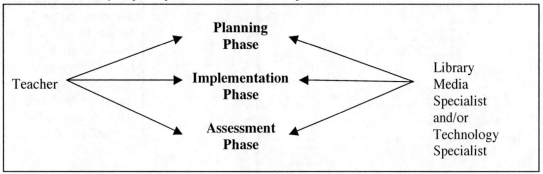

Why is a professional library media specialist and/or technology specialist an essential part of collaboration?

The library media and technology specialists have:

Knowledge of the curriculum, teaching, and learning.

Education (these persons often holds teacher credentials plus a library media credential or masters degree in educational technology).

Experience working with teachers, learners, and materials.

Tools and materials expertise (knows the right tool and information source for the right person at the right time).

Knowledge of techniques for using technology to enhance learning.

A repertoire of successful practices with a wide variety of teachers, students, and technologies — thus serving as an idea fountain.

Knowledge of student achievement over time.

The bottom line:
When professionals collaborate to implement a quality learning experience, the odds of success are doubled.

Indiana Academic Standards and Indicators

Indiana, under the direction of the Indiana General Assembly, has developed new academic standards to prepare students for the future. The standards describe what a student should know and be able to do in each subject, at each grade level. They outline a connected body of understandings and competencies, and are a comprehensive foundation that all students should learn.

READING THE STANDARDS AT EACH GRADE LEVEL

Each English/Language Arts Standard includes the following components to aid teachers in understanding the Standards and incorporating them into their instruction:

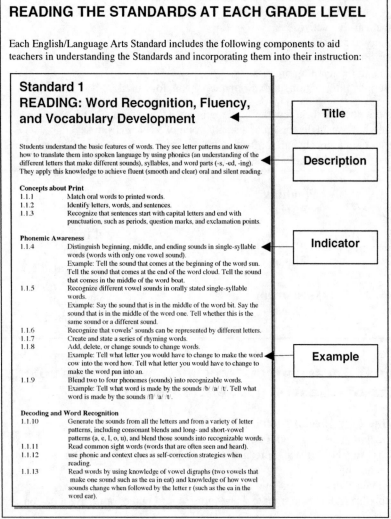

Standard 1
READING: Word Recognition, Fluency, and Vocabulary Development ◄——— **Title**

Students understand the basic features of words. They see letter patterns and know how to translate them into spoken language by using phonics (an understanding of the different letters that make different sounds), syllables, and word parts (-s, -ed, -ing). They apply this knowledge to achieve fluent (smooth and clear) oral and silent reading. ◄——— **Description**

Concepts about Print
1.1.1   Match oral words to printed words.
1.1.2   Identify letters, words, and sentences.
1.1.3   Recognize that sentences start with capital letters and end with punctuation, such as periods, question marks, and exclamation points.

Phonemic Awareness
1.1.4   Distinguish beginning, middle, and ending sounds in single-syllable words (words with only one vowel sound). ◄——— **Indicator**
          Example: Tell the sound that comes at the beginning of the word sun. Tell the sound that comes at the end of the word cloud. Tell the sound that comes in the middle of the word boat.
1.1.5   Recognize different vowel sounds in orally stated single-syllable words.
          Example: Say the sound that is in the middle of the word bit. Say the sound that is in the middle of the word one. Tell whether this is the same sound or a different sound.
1.1.6   Recognize that vowels' sounds can be represented by different letters.
1.1.7   Create and state a series of rhyming words.
1.1.8   Add, delete, or change sounds to change words.
          Example: Tell what letter you would have to change to make the word ◄——— **Example**
          cow into the word how. Tell what letter you would have to change to make the word pan into an.
1.1.9   Blend two to four phonemes (sounds) into recognizable words.
          Example: Tell what word is made by the sounds /b/ /a/ /t/. Tell what word is made by the sounds /f/ /a/ /t/.

Decoding and Word Recognition
1.1.10   Generate the sounds from all the letters and from a variety of letter patterns, including consonant blends and long- and short-vowel patterns (a, e, I, o, u), and blend those sounds into recognizable words.
1.1.11   Read common sight words (words that are often seen and heard).
1.1.12   use phonic and context clues as self-correction strategies when reading.
1.1.13   Read words by using knowledge of vowel digraphs (two vowels that make one sound such as the ea in eat) and knowledge of how vowel sounds change when followed by the letter r (such as the ea in the word ear).

Each standard is a broad statement of an expectation. Students will be successful when their classroom instruction focuses on the standards. The goal is for all students to meet the expectations described in the standards. Indicators are age-appropriate concepts for each standard. These ideas build a foundation for understanding the intent of each standard. The indicators represent a student's performance and signify growth or progress toward meeting the standard. Indicators offer guidelines for what students should know and be able to do to achieve the standard.

Example: First grade students, each of whom had read over 200 library books before the end of the first semester, chose their top ten favorites. Then, in a play for their parents, they dressed up as book characters, retold the stories to the audience, and then showcased, after each telling their phonics skills by using words from the books they could now read.

Using Indiana Standards and Correlation Documents

Under the Indiana General Assembly's direction, world-class standards that are clear, concise, jargon-free, and by grade level were created in 2001. These standards created as a part of Public Law 221 link expectations for what each learner is to know and be able to do with the statewide ISTEP+ assessments that measure performance.

For library media specialists and technology specialists, four publications constitute the complete set of guides to the Indiana standards movement and should be studied carefully as background for collaborative work in the curriculum.

Standards. The actual list of standards for each curricular area and all grade levels is available online at: http://www.doe.state.in.us/standards. This list contains only the standards and indicators.

Teacher's Editions of Standards. Each of the curricular areas for which standards have been developed, the teacher's edition contains the standards, the indicators and examples of how students might demonstrate their competence.

Curriculum Frameworks. Frameworks documents for each curricular

are "handbooks" that offer sample lesson ideas that can be used to meet the standards. Use of the sample lessons is not required, nor do they replace local creativity, but provide idea starters. For technology specialists, the frameworks are important because tips for incorporating technology across the curriculum are woven into each lesson suggested in the frameworks.

Information Literacy Correlations. To assist the library media specialists of the state, the School Library Media Specialists' Leadership Cadre, Information Literacy Task Force Committee has developed correlation documents for various curricular areas that list each of the standards and their indicators for that curriculum and provide a handy checklist of which of the nine information literacy standards might be taught as a part of that standard and indicator.

Thus, in a planning meeting, teachers, library media specialists, and technology specialists might begin with the following questions:
1. What **standards** will we be teaching?
2. What **assessments** will we be using? (Will these assessments reflect the **indicators** listed in the standards?)
3. What **teaching ideas** from the Frameworks might help in our planning?
4. What **technology ideas** from the frameworks might assist our learners?
5. What **information literacy** skills from the correlation documents would be helpful to our learners?

Integrating State Standards/Curriculum Goals in the Planning of a Library Media Center Activity

Every year, it seems that another agenda, list, skill, directive, or standard is required to be integrated into the various units of instruction taught without increasing the amount of time. At times it seems overwhelming. Realistically, in most schools, there will only be a few occasions during the year to plan in-depth with the library media specialist. Try the following approach:

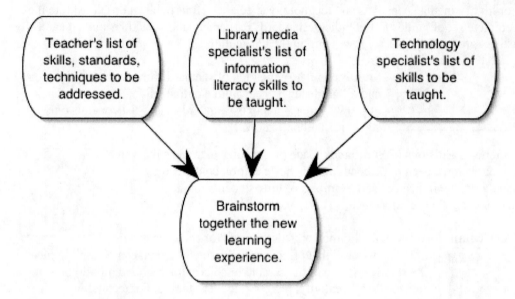

Challenges:

> How can we overlay everyone's goals without increasing the amount of time for the learning experience beyond what is reasonable?
> What activities have we done in the past that could be streamlined or eliminated giving more time for more important learning activities?
> Can we redesign in such a way that motivation and engagement are heightened?

Questions to consider:

> Can information-finding time in the library media center be compressed allowing learners more time to read, think, synthesize, and conclude?
> Can student reports be compressed, eliminated, or transformed into more meaningful learning products?
> As learners read, view and listen, can they not only take notes but concept map as they go (forcing them to focus on the major ideas)?
> How can the amount of time creating the hi-tech product be compressed so learners concentrate on content, not the technology? Is a low-tech product just as productive and less time-consuming?

What to Do Before You Plan: Tips for Library Media Specialists and Technology Specialists

Being prepared to be an excellent collaborative partner is a must if library media specialists and technology specialists are to be credible. The following checklist and planning diagram might help.

Before you plan:

- ❑ Understand Indiana academic standards to be covered.
- ❑ Do some reading in the content area if you are unfamiliar with the content.
- ❑ Have a "How to build a question" tip sheet available.
- ❑ Have your bag of learning activity tricks ready.
- ❑ Anticipate technology and software that might help learners.
- ❑ Anticipate blocks of time for LMC and computers.
- ❑ Analyze the information literacy tasks that are a part of the proposed Indiana academic standard to be taught.
- ❑ Anticipate connections to outside information and technology resources.
- ❑ Have a rubric construction tool available for learner assessment.

Strategy during planning:

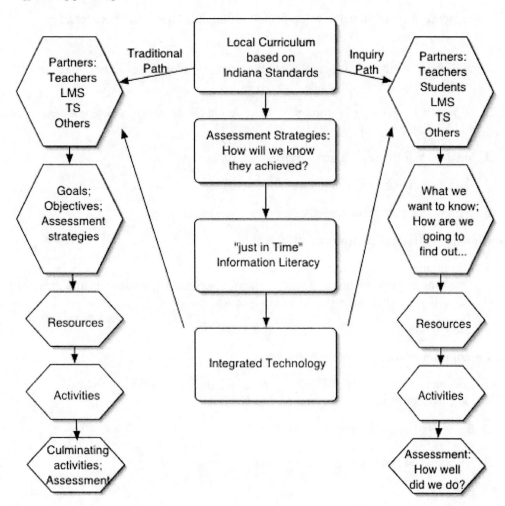

Teacher/Library Media Specialist and Technology Specialist Collaboration: What It Looks Like

If teachers, library media specialists and technology specialists were collaborating successfully to build quality learning experiences, what an observer would see:

Teachers, library media specialists and technology specialists are:

❑ Brainstorming a curricular unit.

❑ Developing plans, activities, and assessments for a learning experience.

❑ Choosing the materials and technologies to support instruction.

❑ Working side by side as the unit activities happen.

❑ Jointly evaluating the success of the unit.

❑ Engaging in professional development to refine the collaborative process.

Learners are:

❑ Working in a bustling, learning lab atmosphere, on projects, problem solving, portfolios, presentations, and assignments.

❑ Using a wide variety of information sources and information technologies from print to multimedia to digital.

❑ Sharing their findings in group-related activities.

❑ Engaging in learning with interest and excitement.

❑ Working by themselves quietly on projects or research.

Library media center and computer facilities are:

❑ Functioning to support individuals, small groups, and large groups for quiet individual study, information gathering, busy production activities, group work, and presentations as the collaborative process begins to produce results.

❑ Rarely empty.

Library media center and school networks are:

❑ Brimming with **quality** information streaming throughout the library media center, into the classrooms, and into the home.

❑ Being used and used and used.

❑ Available 24 hours a day, 7 days a week.

❑ Reliable.

Collaborative Unit Planning, Sheet 1

Teacher/LMS/TS team: _____

Content area: _____

Unit of Study: _____

Unit planning began (date): _____ **Unit ended (date):** _____

LMC Use dates: _____ **Computer Lab dates:** _____

Goals and Objectives / Essential questions of the Unit:

Proposed Learning Activities and Products:

State Academic Standard:

Information Literacy Skills:

- ☐ IS1: Access information efficiently/effectively
- ☐ IS2: Evaluate information critically/competently
- ☐ IS3: Use information accurately/creatively
- ☐ IS4: Personal interest
- ☐ IS5: Creative Expression
- ☐ IS6: Knowledge generation/Independent learning
- ☐ IS7: Importance of info in democratic society
- ☐ IS8: Ethical behavior in regard to info and technology
- ☐ IS9: Collaboration with others

Integrated Technologies:

Responsibilities: (for each, mark T= Teacher, LMS= Library Media Specialist; TS = Technology Specialist; S = Student; A = All)

How Will We Assess Learning?

What Happened? (list activities as they occur)

Example: mini-lesson on how to judge currency of information (teacher and LMS taught)

Print p. 33 and 34 back to back and then attach additional sheets if needed..

Collaborative Unit Evaluation
(TO BE FILLED IN AS A COLLABORATIVE TEAM)

Unit title: _____

Total time spent by LMS/TS:_____ # Students affected: _____

What worked well in the unit?

Suggestions for improvement:

(Time spent on Info. Lit. Teaching/Technology:_____)
(as a subset of the total time listed above)

How well were state academic Standards met? (List by St.#)

Information literacy skills learned:
- ☐ IS2: Evaluate information critically/competently
- ☐ IS3: Use information accurately/creatively
- ☐ IS4: Personal interest
- ☐ IS5: Creative Expression
- ☐ IS6: Knowledge generation/Independent learning
- ☐ IS7: Importance of info in democratic society
- ☐ IS8: Ethical behavior in regard to info and technology
- ☐ IS9: Collaboration with others

Technology impact:

From both the teacher's and library media/technology specialist's points of view, was this unit enhanced through collaboration?
        ☐ Yes   ☐ No   Why?

Was the unit successful enough to warrant doing it again in the future?
        ☐ Yes   ☐ No   Why?

Results of grade or rubrics evaluation of student performance:

This page could be the back of p. 33

Collaborative Unit Planning, Sheet 2[1]

LMS/TS: _____   Date _____

Teacher/Team _____   Class Size _____

Content Area _____   Unit of Study _____

Students in Library (Date(s)/Time)_____

Planning Sessions (Date(s)/Time _____   Evaluation Session (Date/Time) _____

Content Standard(s) Addressed – List all that apply: (Example: 6.1.36; 6.1.45; 6.4.8)

Information literacy standard(s) addressed – Check all that apply:

❑	IS1 Access information efficiently/effectively	❑	IS6: Knowledge generation/Independent learning
❑	IS2: Evaluate information critically/competently	❑	IS7: Importance of info in democratic society
❑	IS3: Use information accurately/creatively	❑	IS8: Ethical behavior in regard to info and technology
❑	IS4: Personal interests	❑	IS9: Collaboration with others
❑	IS5: Creative Expression		

Proposed Activities/Responsibilities: (T = Teacher, LMS – Library media Specialist) TS = Technology Specialist)
(Example: Review outlining – T   Explain info needed for bibliography – LMS Demo use of EL/Newsbank – LMS/TS)

Proposed Outcome/Product: (Example: Students will take notes, prepare an outline and produce a 4-8 paragraph report. Students will learn how to use Newsbank and other electronic information sources with a strict eye for quality.)

Assessment: (Example: Report rubric)

Evaluation of Collaborative Plan: (Use any of the following as needed)
❑ Did this project have the intended outcomes?
❑ What worked well?
❑ Were there enough appropriate materials/sources available in the Library Media Center/ Computer Lab
   o   What additional materials/technology are needed?
   o   What outdated materials need to be withdrawn?
❑ Was the unit enhanced through collaboration?
❑ Total time spent by LMS? Teacher? Technology Specialist?
   o   What amount of that time was spent on information skills?
❑ Is the unit worth doing again?

_____

[1] Thanks to Cheryl Wilson, Fegely Middle School, Portage, IN

4R's Lesson Plan[1]

Grade Level (Circle):   K   1   2   3   4   5   6

Corp Name _____   School Name _____

Content Areas Addressed		Indiana Academic Standards	
Indicators and /or Learning Goals Addressed			
Essential Questions			

Assessment and Evaluation

How the learning goals or essential goals will be assessed?	
How the learning goals or essential goals will be evaluated?	

Instructional Development: Time Frame: How many hours or days? _____

Guiding Questions	
Stage 1 –	
Stage 2 –	
Stage 3 –	
Learning Resources: Technology resources, media resources, books, web sites, www.inspire.net, http://marcopolo.worldcom.com	
Collaborative Partners: Media specialist, technology specialist, other teachers, community resource people	

---

[1] Indiana Web Academy form. At: http://4r.indianawebacademy.org

Ban the "Bird" Units From the Library Media Center and the Computer Lab!

There are certain uses of the library media center and technology that contribute little or nothing to learning. The design team should recognize the flaws and recreate the learning experience.

What is a "bird" unit?

A common pattern:
1. The teacher provides background to a topic in the classroom (could be birds, presidents, countries, states, people, etc.).
2. Textbook work is done.
3. The teacher asks class to do a project in the library media center or computer lab and provides a worksheet for data collection. The worksheet contains fact questions.
4. Students pick a "bird" to research and go to the LMC or lab where the library media specialist or computer teacher introduces them to a few resources.
5. Students copy information from information sources onto their papers.
6. Students report back to the class or turn the papers in for a grade.

Why is a "bird" unit generally a disaster?

When the emphasis of research work in the library media center or computer lab is merely the cutting and clipping of information into some sort of report and then presenting those facts, little learning takes place. In the age of technology, students can easily cut and clip megabytes of information from the Internet or electronic sources and turn them in as a report. In such cases, time in the library media center or the computer lab is wasted and little progress toward educational achievement is made. In fact, assignments like these encourage plagiarism.

What is to be done?

1. Re-design the unit so learners must THINK ABOUT THE INFORMATION they collect, thus increasing learning and achievement.

2. Re-design so that learners must DO SOMETHING with the information they collect such as sense-making, performing, trying out, acting, building, etc.

3. Cut and clip is an *adult* problem as much as it is a *student* problem. Re-designing until it doesn't happen is a fascinating challenge.

Building a Better "Bird" Unit

Generally, a small change in the structure of a unit plan can do wonders for learning. Here is one example to consider. Can a better one be created?

Old "bird" unit:

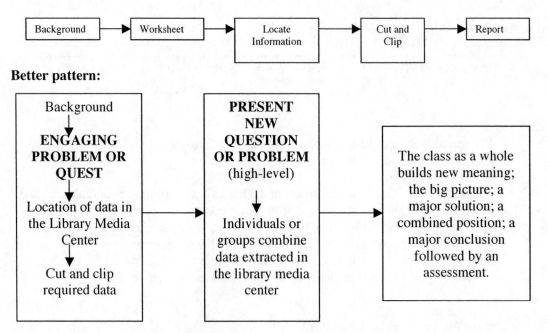

| Background | → | Worksheet | → | Locate Information | → | Cut and Clip | → | Report |

Better pattern:

Background
↓
ENGAGING PROBLEM OR QUEST
↓
Location of data in the Library Media Center
↓
Cut and clip required data

→

PRESENT NEW QUESTION OR PROBLEM (high-level)
↓
Individuals or groups combine data extracted in the library media center

→

The class as a whole builds new meaning; the big picture; a major solution; a combined position; a major conclusion followed by an assessment.

In the above pattern, students are required to combine, manipulate, or rearrange the data they collect, causing them to think about what they have collected in order to solve the problem at hand. In other words, they fit the puzzle pieces they have collected into a large puzzle to discover what the whole picture looks like. The table below shows an example of the illustration above. The research of the first groups leads to a tougher question for the second groupings.

First groups of novices

Question:
What is the difference between the parts of a human and the parts of a bird?

Parts of the Bird Research Groups: wings vs. arms, feathers vs. body hair, bone structure.

Second groupings of mini-experts: one from each novice group
Question:
Why can birds fly and humans can't?

The BIG Answer
It requires the expertise of all groups to answer the question. The answer might lead to a new question: Why don't all birds fly?

Sample Better "Bird" Units to Try in the LMC

There are generally two strategies that work well to transform a low-level activity into a higher level one:

> Change the question (the task or quest).
> Change the product at the end.

Traditional Information activities	More Challenging Information Activities
Complete a worksheet of facts about a state.	Brainstorm questions they want answered about a state, or, "If a wall were constructed around the state, could it survive on its own?"
Read facts about a subject and take a multiple choice test on the subject.	Working in small groups, students create a word web about a topic.
Listen to a lecture about World War II (or some other war).	Interview veterans for a report comparing effects of wars on the country: Korea, Vietnam, World War II, or the Gulf War.
Copy information about pollution from a Power Point presentation.	Students design and conduct a survey to gather information about pollution in the community, the results of which will be presented to a city board or council.
Answer teacher-prepared questions about a community problem.	Students explore their community and prepare a list of community problems needing a solution for a city councilman.
Write an essay about what you did last summer.	Suppose you went to your closet in the morning and found that your clothes had been replaced with various theatrical costumes? Describe your day.
Do a report about the environment.	What should happen to the ugly, smelly swamp next to the school grounds?; Suppose we discovered that this school was built on a toxic dump. What would have to happen?
Make a report on how a bill becomes a law.	Propose a law to the city/county/state government and start it through the political process (through proposal, to enactment, to defeat).
Solve these problems on area. (Math)	The building engineer needs to know how much paint to order to paint this classroom. What is our best advice?
Make graphs and charts using this set of numbers.	Chart and graph high and low temperatures for our town this week compared with a distant city where someone you know lives.

Question: What was the most exciting question or problem you worked on during your own K-12 years? Why do you remember it?

Collaborative Unit Planning Sheet
Grades K-4 Example[1]

Teachers/Team: Grade 3 teachers
LMS/TS:
Content Area: Mathematics
Unit Planning Beginning Date: April 10
      Ending Date: April 15
Goals & Objectives/Essential Quest. of the Unit:
1. Students utilize problem solving skills in a Variety of situations

2. Students apply the Big6 skills to everyday life.

3. Students can create Kidspiration documents Reflecting their problem solving patterns.

State Academic Standards:

Mathematics Standard 6
Problem Solving

Information Literacy Skills:

Standard 1 Accesses Information

Standard 2 Evaluates Information
Standard 3 Uses Information
Standard 4 Pursues Information
Standard 5 Appreciates Information
Standard 6 Generates Knowledge

NETS Standards:

Standard 1 Basic Operations & Concepts
Standard 6 Problem –Solving & Decision Making Tools

Proposed Learning Activities (in order of occurrence),
Needed Equipment, Products, and Assessments,
Responsibilities: (T = Classroom Teacher, LMS = Library Media Specialist,
TS = Technology Specialist, S = Students, A = All)

Activity	Materials/ Equipment	Product	Assessment	Responsible Person
1. Read alouds showing characters needing to problems solve	Books			T
2. Big6 overview	Big6 Poster			LMS/TS
3. T and LMS/TS demonstrate how literature characters' problems can be put into the Big6 format.	Books Big6 Poster Kidspiration Computers	Kidspiration document		A
4. In pairs, students choose books and create Kidspiration document showing literature characters' problem solving	Books Kidspiration Computers	Kidspiration document	Rubric	S
5. Students apply Big6 to personal problem and show process in Kidspiration	Big6 Poster Kidspiration Computers	Kidspiration document	Rubric	S

---

[1] Thanks to Noblesville Schools for this example.

Collaborative Unit Planning Sheet
Grades 5-8 Example[1]

Teachers/Team: Grade 7 Science teachers
LMS/TS:
Content Area: Science
Unit Planning Beginning Date: Sept. 9
      Ending Date: Sept 12
Goals & Objectives/Essential Quest of the Unit:
1. Students utilize and evaluate websites and search engines to decide which best suits their needs.

2. Students apply efficient searching techniques.

3. Students discern differences in websites. Students share why they think a particular search engine/website meets a specific need for assigned topics

State Academic Standards:

Science Standard 1

Nature of science and Technology

Information Literacy Skills:

Standard 1 Accesses Information

Standard 2 Evaluates Information

Standard 3 Uses Information
Standard 4 Pursues Information

Standard 5 Appreciates Information
Standard 6 Generates Knowledge

Standard 7 Recognizes Info. Imp.

Standard 8 Practices Ethical Behavior

Standard 9 Shares and Collaborates

NETS Standards:

Standard 1 Basic Oper. & Concepts
Standard 2 Social, ethical...Issues
Standard 3 Productivity Tools
Standard 4 Communication Tools
Standard 5 Research Tools
Standard 6 Problem-Solving...Tools

**Proposed Learning Activities (in order of occurrence),
Needed Equipment, Products, and Assessments,
Responsibilities: (T = Classroom Teacher, LMS = Library Media Specialist,
TS = Technology Specialist, S = Students, A = All)**

Activity	Materials/ Equipment	Product	Assessment	Responsible Person
1. Introduction of Science Standards 7.1.1-7.1.4	Books			T
2. Introduction of Search Engines	Computers			LMS/TS
3. Students Compare Computer Search Engines	Computers	Chart	**Completed Chart**	A
4. Overview of Initial Topics				T
5. Introduction of Searching Strategies	Computers	Kidspiration document	Rubric	LMS/TS
6. Students Record Results of Search	Computers	Chart	Completed Chart	A

---

[1] Thanks to Noblesville Schools for this example.

Collaborative Unit Planning Sheet
Grades 9 – 12 Sample[1]

Teachers/Team: Grade 10 English teachers
LMS?TS:
Content Area: English
Unit Planning Beginning Date: November 4
Ending Date: November 9

Goals & Objectives/Essential Questions of the Unit:

1. Students read and evaluate a variety of expository writings as described in English Standard 10.2.4.

2. Students write a coherent thesis as described in English Standard 10.4.2.

State Academic Standards:
English Standard 2
Reading: Reading Comprehension
English Standard4
Writing: Writing Process

Information Literacy Skills:
Standard 2 Evaluates Information
Standard 3 Uses Information
Standard 4 Pursues Information
Standard 5 Appreciates Information
Standard 6 Generates Knowledge
Standard 9 Shares and Collaborates

NETS Standards:
Standard 3 Productivity Tools
Standard 4 Communications Tools

Proposed Learning Activities (in order of occurrence), Needed Equipment, Products, and Assessments.
Responsibilities: (T=Classroom Teacher, LMS=Library Media Specialist, TS=Technology Specialist, S=Student, A=All)

Activity	Materials/Equipment	Product	Assessment	Responsible Person
1. Students hear good expository writing samples read aloud	Expository writing			CT & LMS
2. Students will read and discuss expository writing	Expository writing			S
3. Students will draft an essay about a topic important to them.	Computers Quote Books	Essay draft		S
4. Students will use reference material to support their ideas.	Computers Reference Materials	Bibliography		A
5. The writing process will be used to take the piece to publication	Computers Peer Editors	Essay Draft	Rubric	A

---

[1] Thanks to Noblesville Schools for this example.

Reading Your Way Through an Instructional Unit With the Help of the Library Media Center

Problem: Many learners in the class either do not know English well or do not read well.

One idea to test: Have students read their way through a topical unit.

Step one: With the library media specialist, present the major question, standard, and concept the learners should understand.

Step two: Introduce tons of reading, viewing, and listening materials (book talks, descriptions, annotated bibliography). Make these materials available in the classroom and on line. Be sure that these materials are non-standard, i.e., including many pictorial sources, high interest-low vocabulary, timelines, comic book-type resources, charts, graphs, maps, models, realia, fascinating web sites, faction (fictional treatment of factual topics such as historical fiction), etc.

Step Three: Spend a chunk of time (2-3 full class periods or more) having everyone read, view or listen. As they do so, have them keep brief notes and at the last 10 minutes do a mind map.

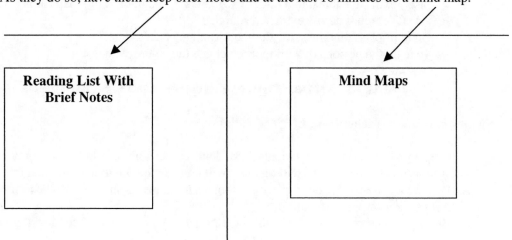

Reading List With Brief Notes

Mind Maps

Alternate Step Three: As students read, they might keep notes such as:

Major Concept in My Reading	Why It Is Important	My Reaction

Step Four: Hold a discussion, an exploration, compare/contrast challenge on a high-level question reflective of the major standard or concept of the unit.

Step Five: Do the normal assessment. How do learners perform? How did the poor readers or low-English learners do?

Rx for Cut and Clip

Problem: Are learners cutting and clipping facts, paragraphs, articles, complete term papers from library books, periodicals, Internet sites and turning them in as their own work? Perhaps they have become creative and "dress up" the appearance of what they find and then turn it in. The bottom line is that they do very little thinking or learning. It's a zero educational experience!

Rx: With the library media and technology specialists, build better questions for learners; have learners build better questions for themselves. The definition of a better question is one that cannot be answered through cut and clip mentality.

Examples:

Invitations to cut and clip:
➢ A list of fact questions to answer.
➢ An assignment where the "answer" is easily located in a periodical article, a book, or a web site.

Challenges to think:
➢ Compare/contrast two opinion pieces.
➢ Insert extracted data into a larger matrix, chart, diagram, mind map for analysis.
➢ Look for trends across extracted sources.
➢ Build in-class timelines, look at the meaning, cause/effect.
➢ Take on the persona of an important character; re-enact an event.

Ideas for Other Opportunities and Challenges

Suggestions when teachers and LMS/TS collaborate:

➢ Create good and clear assignments so students can begin immediately and stay engaged.
➢ Include creative uses of technology that will contribute both to learning and interest.
➢ Require a wide variety of information sources to help students explore the rich world of information across the media.
➢ Build the research process into the whole project so that students keep making progress toward becoming independent and more sophisticated learners over time.
➢ Build in reflection along the way to help students assess what they know, and how efficient their strategies are.

Activities Likely to Fail

➢ Spur-of-the-moment activities with little notice given to the LMS/TS.
➢ Unclear assignments or directions to learners, causing them to waste time, become behavior problems, or wander in a state of stupor.
➢ Competition for scarce information resources (when every other teacher is having students research the same topic at the same time).
➢ Assignments that do not require evaluation of information sources (You will get back information copied from the first hit on an Internet search, facts copied from an out-of-date reference source, and other nonsense mindlessly regurgitated).

Pacing the Library Media Center Activity: It Can Make All the Difference!

Pacing a learning activity is critical if deep learning is to be elevated. We are all familiar with searching, retrieving, procrastinating, and doing the final project the night before it is due. Helping learners manage the learning task focuses emphasis on reading, analyzing, synthesizing, concluding, and metacognitive tasks. Building checkpoints can help change the schedule as illustrated below.

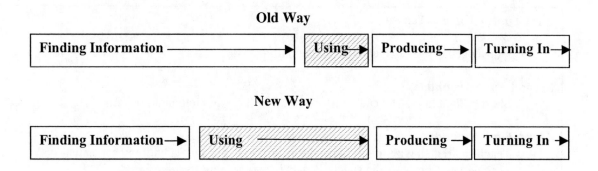

Another streamline of the learning activity as a whole might be to look for certain activities that consume time without retuning significant learning and replacing that time with an activity holding more promise. Consider the suggestion below:

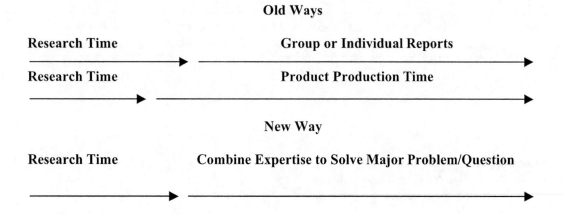

Building a Repertoire of Collaborative Projects With the Teachers

Let's face it, there are many teachers and few library media and technology specialists. If every unit were jointly planned, implemented, and assessed as a team, the library media and technology specialists would burn out in a week. Nevertheless, teachers will want to take every opportunity to collaborate. One strategy for the library media and technology specialists to stay alive is to collaborate, release; collaborate, release. Consider the following:

First Time a Topic is Taught:

Plan Together ⟶ Team Implementation ⟶ Assess ⟶ Revise

Second Time Around:
Shorter Planning ⟶ Teacher More/LMS-TS Less Implementation Time ⟶ Assess

Third Time Around:
Teacher-directed with minimal need for library media and technology specialists
Teacher and library media specialist tackle another unit for redesign
Etc., Etc., Etc.

Consider a second model designed to spread the library media specialist's services:

Use model one except ask the library media and technology specialists to collaborate with a group of teachers rather than an individual (a grade level, department, existing team, etc.).

Warning: All planned units get stale!
> ➤ **Poor**: Plan once, teach many times.
> ➤ **Better:** Plan once, teach a few times; revise and rejuvenate

Why Keep Collaborating?

What are the essential reasons for the teachers and the library media and technology professionals to keep working together, building good relationships, retrying when relationships may become strained, and just building consistency over time?

Checklist:

❑ Every time we collaborate there is a lower teacher/pupil ratio for the unit.

❑ Collaboration capitalizes on twice the teaching experience.

❑ There is a peer available to "evaluate" plans.

❑ We combine creative ideas with a realistic sense of what will work.

❑ Collaboration maximizes productivity.

❑ We split the workload.

❑ During collaboration, we encourage each other when things get tough.

❑ We provide support if and when needed.

❑ When there are funds for materials and information resources, collaborative partners usually get higher priority.

❑ It would be difficult to do worse than if either collaborative partner tried to "go it alone."

❑ We can draw upon each other's native abilities and strengths.

❑ Discipline problems are cut in half.

❑ If students don't do as well academically as we thought, we redesign until we get the results we expect.

❑ There is more time to deal with individual student differences, abilities, learning styles, etc.

❑ We can devote more time to helping each student succeed.

❑ Your reasons:

A Teacher's Share: Working the LMC
Schedule to Their Advantage

Not all units of instruction lend themselves to an information-rich or high-tech environment. The teacher and the LMC professionals are wise to choose a few learning experiences where collaboration is likely to maximize learning. Consider the following questions designed to help select the best units for collaboration.

> ➢ What units would flourish in an information-rich environment?

> ➢ What units are better taught in depth rather than breadth?

> ➢ Which topics lend themselves to "two heads are better than one?"

> ➢ How can I space the collaborations across the year to provide the best variety of learning experiences for the students of a particular teacher, grade level, or department? Would this collaboration schedule provide for increased sophistication in the use of technology and in information literacy across the year?

Sample topics that might be better in the library media center:

> ➢ **A topic where issues, opinions, or positions are central to the main concept.** (Human cloning, Arab/Israeli conflict, community issues, state or national elections, what foods help prevent heart disease?)

> ➢ **Topics where the textbook coverage is so sparse that learners cannot develop enough background knowledge or depth of knowledge to count for anything.** (Rain forest, Vietnam War, why a particular novel was a landmark of its time, the impact of scientific learning on culture, What causes people such as the Pilgrims to embark on huge journeys?, Why did it take mathematicians 400 years to figure out how to calculate longitude? [trick question], How does art seem to reflect the society of its time?)

> ➢ **Topics where lots of individual learner choice in exploration would increase motivation.** (Learners can read a wide variety of materials on a topic – at their level; a favorite dinosaur can be explored in depth; my own career interest can be explored in depth; my interest in particular sports and sports figures can be pursued; issues I feel strongly about can be illuminated.)

> ➢ **Topics lending themselves to creative expression.** (recreating a period drama to get the historical setting right, retelling the Cinderella story from many cultures, comparing performances of a piece of music across time as we create our own interpretation, recreating cultural artifacts)

Flexible Access to Resources

Ask elementary school library media specialists and computer lab teachers in the United States to identify their biggest problem and they will say that once-a-week scheduled visits <u>prevent</u> them from having a major impact on academic achievement. Library media specialists and computer lab teachers often have their jobs because they are funded or are under union contract as planning time for elementary teachers. In many schools, the weekly visit schedule ties up the most expensive laboratory space in the school almost the entire week. Individuals, small groups, and other classes needing to use the facility for curricular activities are denied access. The profession advocates the abandonment of "rigid schedules" in favor of flexible ones. That is, the library media center/computer lab should be open all day every day. Individuals and small groups can come at any time. And classes can be scheduled for research when teachers and library media specialists want to collaborate. Many schools combine the LMC and computer lab into a single flexibly-scheduled facility.

What are the advantages of the flexible schedule?

➢ The LMC becomes a learning laboratory available to everyone throughout the school day.

➢ Library media specialists have time to collaborate with teachers to create enhanced learning experiences – something that the research shows is the best predictor of increased academic achievement.

➢ The LMC responds to the curriculum, not the curriculum to the LMC.

➢ Library media specialists teach information literacy at the point of need rather than a less effective "course of instruction" – another factor showing greater increases in achievement.

➢ Teachers can schedule the "learning lab" to fit into their unit schedule – sometimes every day for several days and not at all other days. And they can schedule the library media specialist, their partner teacher, for projects when two teachers would be better than one.

➢ Students can get to the LMC when they need it – not just once a week.

If you absolutely must retain the weekly schedule:

➢ Demand that individuals, small groups, and large groups can use the LMC/lab whether or not a scheduled class is there. Arrange the LMC/lab facility so this can happen.

➢ Consider having classes scheduled every other week rather than once a week to free up the LMC/lab schedule for collaborative units.

➢ Consider having the scheduled class do sustained silent reading (SSR) and book checkout during their scheduled visits to the LMC. The library media specialist would be working with other classes simultaneously on research projects. Have support staff supervise the SSR activity.

➢ See that more and more information is available on networks to classrooms and homes.

What if flexible scheduling is not working?

➢ Send a library media specialist/computer lab and a group of teachers to a place where it is working for a day of analysis and planning.

➢ Pilot the new plan with a few teachers first, then the school as a whole.

THE BOTTOM LINE

The library media center or computer lab are a very expensive investments that must pay their way.

Locking it up through rigid schedules negates its impact.

Professional Development and Resources for Collaboration

Indiana Resources:

➢ The **Office of Learning Resources** web site provides 24/7 access to multimedia examples of collaboration projects planned by IN teacher/media specialist teams. Elementary, middle and high school examples include 'Dream Weavers' an elementary multidisciplinary unit and a middle school virtual fieldtrip based on 'To Kill a Mockingbird.' http://doe.state.in.us/media/video/2002collaboration.html

➢ **ICAN:** Individualized Curriculum and Assessment Notebook. Indiana Department of Education. At http://www.ICANtech.com - a web-based software system that manages individualized curriculum, assessment, and analysis through standards-based accountability. Teachers use an elaborate computer program that helps them track what standards they are working on, their progress, and it also provides a reporting mechanism for analysis and for personal assessment of teaching.

➢ **Inspire Teacher Resource Guide,** developed by teams of teachers and media specialists of the Carmel Clay Schools, under a grant from the IDOE office of Learning Resources. The teams collaborated to plan research units, which start with In Academic Standards for both subject/grade level areas and information literacy. Available at http://ideanet.doe.state.us/olr

➢ **Student Inquiry in the Research Process,** developed by Leslie Preddy, media specialist, Perry Meridian Middle School, Indianapolis, outlines the steps teacher and media specialists can take to develop inquiry lessons. Handouts and resources are included. http://ntserver1.msdpt.k12.in.us/etspages/pm/lmc/inquiry/index.htm

➢ **Technology in the Curriculum** is a collection of video stream examples of teaching units developed by IPS educators. A variety of technology is shown including digital cameras and distance learning. Teachers and administrators comment and evaluate the units. A Parent section is also included. http://doe.state.in.us

Other Resources:

➢ American Association of School Librarians provides a current listing of career development and professional development activities at http://www.ala.org/aasl/education_menu.html

➢ Collaborative Units planned by teachers and media specialists of the Lincoln, NE, Public Schools can be seen at http://www.lps.org/instruction/lms/tealea/

➢ Buzzeo, Toni. *Collaborating to Meet Standards: Teacher/Librarian Partnerships for K-6.* Linworth Publishing, 2001. Provides practical examples of how to implement the collaborative process in a variety of situations. The 19 K-6 units are presented in a standardized template that educators can easily adapt. A second title focuses on grades 7-12.

➢ Dorian, Ray and Judy Davies. *Partners in Learning: Students, Teachers, and the School Library.* Englewood, Colorado: Libraries Unlimited, 1998. Clear explanation of the collaboration process accompanied by detailed lessons created by elementary teacher-media specialist teams.

➢ Weisman, Shirley. *Windows into Instructional Collaboration: Information Power in the Real World.* San Jose, CA: Hi Willow Research & Publishing, 2001. Learn how the library media program has raised academic achievement in some CA schools collection of practical suggestions, collected by a library media specialist, explaining how. Designed for self-study, professional development sessions with teacher and library media specialists, and for courses preparing library media specialists.

Assessment of Collaborative Planning

Because the Lance studies[1] made a very strong link between collaboration in the LMC to academic achievement, the measures taken documenting this activity are vital. Collecting, reviewing, and reporting data at the organizational level, the teaching unit level and the learner level will help assess the impact collaboration is ready to make and is making in the school.

Level of Measure	Factor	Sources of Data
Collaboration at the Organization Level	The state of collaboration in the school and district.	❑ Evidence that district and school level administrators support collaborative planning by actions as well as word. ❑ Evidence that time for collaborative planning is built into the school day. ❑ Evidence that clerical and technical help are available to allow professionals to collaboratively plan.
Collaboration at the Learning Unit Level (class interaction and use)	The success that the class and the teacher experience during a unit of instruction both in the classroom and the LMC when collaborative planning is the norm.	❑ Evidence that collaborative logs are kept showing both planning and assessment of learning experiences. ❑ An analysis of collaboration logs showing spread of collaboration through the grade levels, the various disciplines, and through the faculty. ❑ An analysis of rubrics of classes as a whole for units of instruction done collaboratively. How they rate against instructional units done only in the classroom. ❑ "Teacher" to pupil ratio for this learning unit as compared with normal classroom-based instruction.
Collaboration at the Learner Level (as individuals)	Individual progress by each learner as collaborative planning enhances learning experiences.	❑ Rubric score that content knowledge, technology, and information literacy was enhanced through collaboration. ❑ Evidence that an individual learner was more engaged, interested, and motivated than "normal" as the collaboratively-taught unit progressed.

---

[1] Lance, Keith Curry and David Loertscher. *Powering Achievement*. 2nd ed. San Jose, CA: Hi Willow Research & Publishing, 2003.

How Collaborative Activities Can Be Recorded and Assessed Learning Unit Level

Idea: Create a Collaboration Log.

Who: The library media and technology specialists and classroom teacher working as a team.

Activity: Each time there is a major collaborative learning experience jointly planned, executed, and evaluated by the library media specialist and classroom teachers, do the following:

➢ **File collaborative unit planning sheets** (p.33/34 or 35) in a three-ring notebook in some sensible fashion. Only fully developed collaborative activities should be recorded — not every interaction between the library media and technology specialist and the teachers. An electronic record might be preferable.

➢ As the **first page** in the notebook, create **a collaboration log summary page** listing the collaborative activities. See the example on p. 53 and the worksheet on p. 54.

➢ **Principal's Activity:** Using the summary sheet, assess the collaboration log notebook as a whole looking for patterns.

- Who is being served?
- Which grade levels?
- Which departments?
- Which curricular subjects?
- Who is not being served?

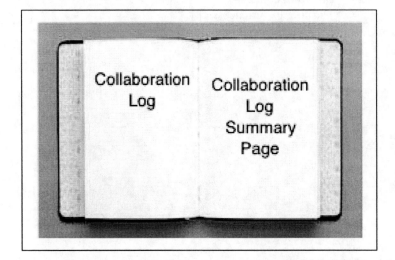

Sample Collaboration Log
Summary Page

During the school year, the teachers and the library media and technology specialists agree that the following units were successful collaborations, i.e., the learning was enhanced because the several partners exploited the resources and technology of the LMC and/or computer lab.

	LMS/TS Time	*#Students*
Social Studies		
Our Local Elections - grade 6 (Smith)	*2.6 hours*	*24*
Family Trees - grades 3 and 4 (Albright and Faire)	*3.6 hours*	*45*
Reading		
Newbery Novel Unit - grades 5 & 6 (Crane & Finch)	*1.5 hours*	*47*
Science		
Environment of the School Grounds - entire school (Principal, LMS and Dwight, leaders)	*15 hours*	*465*
Simple Machines - grade 3 (Truett)	*1.4 hours*	*27*
Nutrition - grades 5 and 6 (Handford and Zigler)	*2.8 hours*	*48*
Integrated Units		
Local Environmental Hazards – Social Studies and Science. gr. 4 (Todd and Lark)	*4.5 hours*	*43*
Labor Movements - SS and Art, grade 6 (Jones and Gregg)	*3.7 hours*	*49*
Totals	*35.1 hours*	*748*

Ideas:

➢ Create a summary chart similar to the one above that details collaborative units taught. Use a single sheet of paper for this summary page. This becomes the first page in the collaboration log.

➢ Create a graphic that summarizes the above list for use in the report.

➢ Enlarge the chart to poster size, use a transparency, or create a PowerPoint presentation when reporting collaborative efforts to the faculty, administration, and the community.

Note to LMS/TS: How many collaborative activities were there? What is the dispersal of collaboration among the faculty, grade levels, and subjects taught? How could I as the instructional leader encourage more and better collaboration? Which of the collaborative activities deserve recognition from the community? How would I assess the effectiveness of increased student learning?

Collaboration Log Summary Page

Time Period Covered _____

The units of instruction listed below are those that the teacher, technology and library media specialists agree were better learning experiences because of the inclusion of LMC resources, technology, and staff.

Category[1]	Unit title (grade level, teacher name)	LMS/TS time	#Students
_____	_____	_____	_____
_____	_____	_____	_____
_____	_____	_____	_____
_____	_____	_____	_____
_____	_____	_____	_____
_____	_____	_____	_____
_____	_____	_____	_____
_____	_____	_____	_____
_____	_____	_____	_____
_____	_____	_____	_____
_____	_____	_____	_____
_____	_____	_____	_____
Totals	_____	_____	_____

Patterns Observed:

Proposed Actions:

_____

[1] Group the list by category in some meaningful way such as by department, grade level topic, etc.

LMC Activity Log[1]   School: _____   Date: From: _____   To: _____

Working with Students (Individuals, Groups, Classes)	Collaboration with Teachers	Curriculum Support	Tech Support / Troubleshooting	LMC Administration	Professional Development	School Committees	Other
Monday							
Tuesday							
Wednesday							
Thursday							
Friday							
TOTAL							

Estimate time in half-hour Increments.

Working with Students – Working directly with, instructing or supervising students individually, in groups or in classes.
Collaboration with Teachers – Planning, preparing assessing, following up activities with individual teachers or teaching teams.
Collaboration Support - Gathering materials, bibliographies, URLs, suggesting materials, resources, etc.
Technology Support / Troubleshooting – Support both inside and outside the library of computers, printers, televisions, etc.; software support
Library Administration – Collection development, book reviews, materials selection, ordering, processing, database maintenance, supervising media aide, etc.
School Committees – Curriculum Alignment, project, PL221, school plan teams, grade-level meetings (Title 1), etc.
Other – Before and after school hours, weekend functions

	Total number of students in classes	Name
		LMS	Aide
Number of classes in the LMC	Total number of students in classes		
Circulation	Number of sign-ins		
	Total number of students		

---

[1] Thanks to Cheryl Wilson, Fegely Middle School, Portage, IN.

BUILDING AVID AND CAPABLE READERS

Reading

The case for readers in the age of information is clear. From *Indiana's Academic Standards: English/Language Arts:*

> *The world is changing fast. In order for students to succeed in school, at work, and in the community, they will need more skills and knowledge than ever before. To meet these challenges, Indiana established new academic standards in English/Language Arts. These world-class standards outline what students should know and be able to do at each grade level… The demand is greater than ever for people who can read, write, speak effectively, analyze problems and set priorities, learn new things quickly, take initiative, and work in teams.*[1]

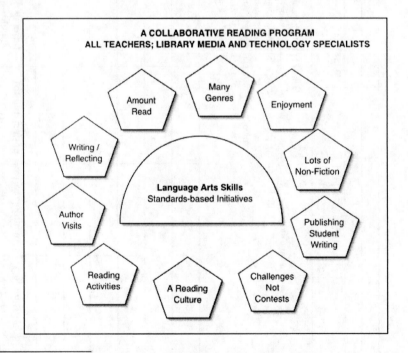

---

[1] *Indiana's Academic Standards: English/Language Arts.* Teacher's Edition. Indianapolis: Indiana Department of Education, 2000, p. i. At http://ideanet.doe.state.in.us/standards/

Literacy *is* a problem to throw money at, but we have to aim carefully by pouring money into library books and then making sure they get read.

—**Stephen Krashen**

Reading Research Linking Reading to Academic Achievement

Research completed by Ann E. Cunningham and Keith E. Stanovich, Stephen Krashen, and Jeff McQuillan plus the latest NAEP research from the U.S. federal government link the amount young people read with their scores on academic achievement. The message is clear:

For Everyone: Amount Counts! One hundred years of research supports the notion that free voluntary reading (the kind of reading you want to do, not have to do) — lots of it — is the best predictor of seven essential achievement basics:

Comprehension, Spelling, Grammar, Vocabulary,
Writing Style, Verbal Fluency, General Knowledge

For English Learners: Amount Counts! Research also demonstrates that the fastest way to get anyone—child, teenager, or adult—to learn English is to have them read a lot in English! (P.S.: this also works with anyone learning a foreign language.)

Reading vs. Television and Adult Conversation. Consider this: 1) Children's books have 50 percent more rare words in them than adult prime-time television, and 2) Popular magazines have roughly three times as many opportunities for new word learning as prime-time television.

The Sources and Must Reads:

> *The Power of Reading* by Stephen Krashen (Libraries Unlimited, 1993).[1]

> *The Literacy Crisis* by Jeff McQuillan (Heinemann, 1998).

> **"What Reading Does for the Mind"** by Ann E. Cunningham and Keith E. Stanovich (*American Educator*, Spring/Summer, 1998, p. 1-8).

> *The Nation's Reading Report Card: Fourth-Grade Reading 2000* by the National Center for Education Statistics, The Center, 2000 (Known popularly as the "NAEP Report").[2]

NAEP Results 2000
Fourth graders in the United States do better academically when they:
> read more pages in school
> read more pages as homework
> have more books, magazines, newspapers, and encyclopedias in their homes
> report that they read for fun every day
> discuss what they read

Do Your Own Preliminary Test: In any group of children or teenagers, ask those who consider themselves avid readers to identify themselves (they read regularly both in and out of school). Compare these students' achievement scores with those who don't consider themselves avid readers.

---

[1] Both Krashen and McQuillan books are available from Language Education Associates, PO Box 3141, Culver City, CA 90231; 800-200-8008; web address: http://www.LanguageBooks.com

[2] The NAEP report is available on the web at http://nces.ed.gov/nationsreporrtcard/sitemap.asp or by doing a web search for the "naep report 2000"

School Libraries: A Legacy of Reading

For as long as there have been school librarians, these professionals have had a main target of building enthusiastic, avid, capable, and interested readers. Tried and true practices in the library world endure, no matter what controversies rage in the "teaching reading" community. What are those tried and true strategies?

> - Storytelling
> - Reading aloud
> - Enjoyment of literature for literature's sake (no book reports, no tests, no critical analysis)
> - Interaction with authors and illustrators
> - Reading motivation activities (state children's choice award programs, Book Week, family reading programs)
> - Collections of great reads for every type of reader
> - Access, access, access to books
> - SSR (sustained silent reading)
> - Pleasant places to read (inviting facilities, ambience, posters, banners, beanbag chairs, bathtubs, reading lofts)
> - Endless booklists and booktalks
> - Adults as model readers who share enthusiasm and favorite titles.
> - Linking readers to other libraries (public, academic)
> - Reader's advisory work (anticipating what a reader will want to read next)
> - Reading celebrations and events

Some ignore or dispute the power of our legacy since its research base is more anecdotal than scientific. Yet it has a wide acceptance across communities, parent groups, and learners of all ages.

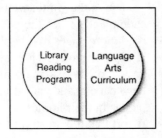

The challenge for the library media specialist and the technology specialist is to preserve the legacy of reading while integrating its aims with those of the language arts curriculum. The library media program is larger in scope in the 21st century than it was thirty years ago. Other agendas such as collaboration, enhancing learning through technology, and information literacy have taken a prominent position in LMC programs. How can the LMC staff preserve the best of the past while pushing toward today's world?

Consider:
> - Take a leadership position in reading rather than conducting a one-person show.
> - Collaborate to achieve both language arts and library reading agendas simultaneously. That is, multitask with activities that accomplish both agendas at the same time.
> - Be a fierce advocate for reading in leadership councils both in school and in the community.
> - Take advantage of the many reading initiatives in the community rather than taking the time and effort to create your own.
> - Demand and lead funding efforts for a large collection of books learners want to read.

Indiana Research on State Spending for Books

> **Improving School Libraries and Independent Reading: 1997-2002 Impact Evaluation of the K-12 School Library Printed Materials Grant**
> Johnathan A. Plucker, Jack Humphrey, Ann M. Kearns, and Chrisanne N. Walter. At:
> http://www2.evansville.edu/mgrnweb/2002readingsurvey.htm

As part of a comprehensive strategy to improve the literacy of Indiana students, the Indiana General Assembly provided $4 million for K-8 schools for the 1997-1999 school years in the School Library Printed Materials Grant. The grant was expanded to K-12 for the second funding cycle (1999-2000 and 2000-2001) and the funds increased to $6 million. Another $6 million was appropriated for a third funding cycle, 2001-2002 and 2002-2003. Due to state financial problems, school corporations received $3 million for the 2001-2002 years and nothing for the second year.

The Middle Grades Reading Network surveyed every public school in the state in 1997 through 2002. Respondents provided both quantitative and qualitative data. Over the four years approximately four books per student were added to collections. Circulation per student rose over the four years from 33.8 to 39.2 per student.

Conclusions	Policy Implications
State funding for school libraries from 1998-2001 resulted in a substantial increase in book purchases and circulation.	The Library Materials Grant Program had a quick and direct impact on the access and quality of materials available to Indiana students, resulting in greater levels of circulation and independent reading.
Book purchasing appears to have a cumulative but potentially short-lived effect on circulation: The reduced level of state funding for school libraries in 2001-2002 resulted in a decline in book purchasing. This decline may explain the relatively small increase in circulation during the most recent school year, 2001-2002.	Lack of targeted funding may erode circulation numbers, eventually impacting reading achievement.
The library materials program appears to be associated with a number of positive student outcomes, including increased use of library materials, increased student ownership of school libraries, higher levels of independent reading, and higher reading achievement.	Despite the state's considerable financial constraints, the role of library materials should be considered in any comprehensive plan to increase the literacy of Indiana's students.
The range of books purchased across all K-8 schools during 2002 is large: Some schools purchased no books, while others purchased many books per student.	Were the program to continue, greater resources should be devoted to program oversight to ensure that the funding is being used to put books in the hands of Indiana's students.

Sample Quote from one library media specialist: "In my nearly 20 years as a library media specialist, I have observed the effects of many different reading incentives. Without a doubt, new books are the most powerful encouragement for reading, especially when those books are titles that students want to read. An increase in book budges guarantees an increase in circulation."

If We Believe the Reading Research, What Should the Teacher and the Library Media Center Provide to:
"Learn to Read"

If a school community really believes the research saying that "amount counts," then the library media center should have an extensive collection of reading materials young people want to read. So many school libraries in the nation have outdated, ragged, and uninteresting reading collections that young people ignore them. When reading collections are large, current, attractive, and easily accessible, good things happen. The best results of library media contributions to reading should be most noticeable when young people have few reading materials in their homes, and when they are in the lowest quartile of reading scores. Is your school library media center program providing the following:

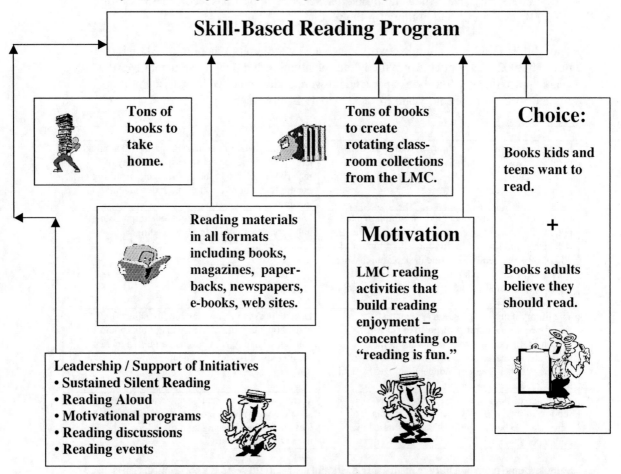

Skill-Based Reading Program

Tons of books to take home.

Tons of books to create rotating class-room collections from the LMC.

Choice:

Books kids and teens want to read.

+

Books adults believe they should read.

Reading materials in all formats including books, magazines, paper-backs, newspapers, e-books, web sites.

Motivation

LMC reading activities that build reading enjoyment – concentrating on "reading is fun."

Leadership / Support of Initiatives
- **Sustained Silent Reading**
- **Reading Aloud**
- **Motivational programs**
- **Reading discussions**
- **Reading events**

Bottom line: The LMC contribution to reading should plug the holes in whatever skill-based program exists toward the goal of 100% avid and capable readers. Does your school's LMC reading program measure up? Are teachers taking advantage of the LMC's resources?

If We Believe the Reading Research, What Should Teachers and the Library Media Center (LMC) Provide to:
"Read to Learn"

As skill in reading builds, the concentration of the reading program shifts to using reading as a tool to learn as well as reading for enjoyment. The library media program has much to contribute to all subject disciplines as content knowledge is expected to mushroom. This will be particularly true in middle schools and high schools where reading is integrated into the entire curriculum and into all departments.

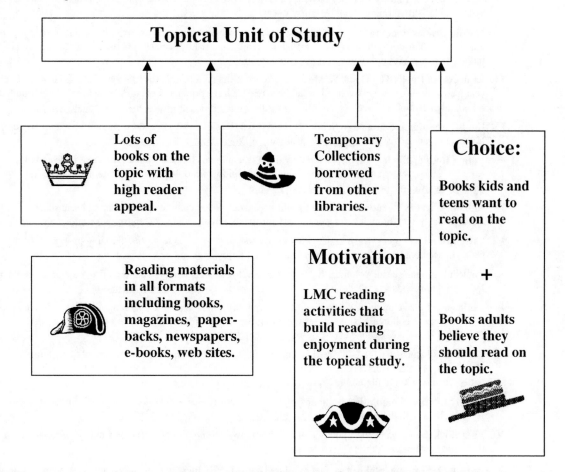

Topical Unit of Study

Lots of books on the topic with high reader appeal.

Temporary Collections borrowed from other libraries.

Choice:

Books kids and teens want to read on the topic.

+

Books adults believe they should read on the topic.

Reading materials in all formats including books, magazines, paper-backs, newspapers, e-books, web sites.

Motivation

LMC reading activities that build reading enjoyment during the topical study.

Bottom line: The LMC contribution to reading in the topical areas should stimulate more expository reading and thus more in-depth knowledge and understanding. Does your school's LMC reading program measure up? Are teachers taking advantage of the LMC's resources when planning their lessons?

Linking to Great Reading Resources

There are so many wonderful reading initiatives locally, in Indiana, and across the nation that the difficulty is choosing those that will enhance and push the local agenda. Below are listed but a few of what is available:

> **O'Bannon Book Buddy** initiative sponsored by the Indiana Literacy Foundation. Sponsored by Indiana Governor Frank O'Bannon and the first lady, Judy O'Bannon, the children of Indiana are encouraged to read a list of titles each month and write about them. Many sponsored events link school to community and to the joy of reading together. At: http://www.IN.gov/bookbuddies/

> **I-READ Literature Lists** provides access to various reading lists including the CARS lists of literature to be read by students at each grade level as correlated to the Indiana academic standards for English/language arts. At http://ideanet.doe.state.in.us/rea/literature.html

> **Star Writers & Family Literacy** provides a variety of writing and literacy projects in Indiana schools beginning in 2001 through 2004. At http://www.buddyproject.org/default.asp

> **Middle Grades Reading Network** provides research, programs, advice, and resources to spur reading in grades 6-8. Their newsletter: *NetWords* is a must read. Directed by Jack Humphrey, this organization is an Indiana treasure! At http://www2.evansville.edu/mgrnweb

> **Read-Aloud Books Too Good To Miss** is a project of the Association for Indiana Media Educators. Each year a committee develops five read-aloud lists, one each for primary school, intermediate school, middle school, high school, and ageless. At http://www.ilfonline.org/Programs/ReadAlous/readaloud.htm

> **Eliot Rosewater Indiana High School Book Award** (Rosie Award) is chosen annually by students across Indiana in grades 9-12. At http://www.ilfonline.org/Programs/Rosie/rosie.htm

> **Young Hoosier Book Award** sponsored by the Association of Indiana Media Educators is designed to stimulate recreational reading among elementary and middle school/junior high school children. At http://www.ilfonline.org/Programs/YHBA/yhba.htm

> **Indiana Literacy Foundation** is a non-profit organization dedication to strengthening basic skills among children and adults through volunteer literacy programs across Indiana. At: http://www.indianaliteracy.org/

> **Civic Literacy Project** works in innovative ways to foster sustainable service-learning programs, positive civic engagement, and educational improvement. At http://serve.indiana.edu

> **BookPals** is a unique all-volunteer literacy program. Professional actors visit public elementary schools in local neighborhoods to read aloud to children every week. At: http://www.bookpals.net

> **Children's Book Council** is a non-profit trade organization dedicated to encouraging literacy and the use of enjoyment of children's books and is the official sponsor of Young People's Poetry Week and Children's Book Week each year. At http://www.cbcbooks.org

> **Children's Literature for Children!** is a nonprofit, educational organization dedicated to bringing children and books together. CLC began in 1972 in Atlanta and provides reader-to-reader, reader-to-patient, and structured literature programs. At http://www.childrensliterature.org/home.html

> **Family Literacy Foundation** facilitates supportive relationships for children through family and friends reading aloud with them. At http://www.read2kids.org/

> **First Book** is an organization giving children from low-income families the opportunity to read and own their first new books. At http://www.firstbook.org

> **Reading is Fundamental** helps deliver children's and family literacy programs that help prepare young children for reading and motivate school-age children to read regularly through book give-away programs, reading challenges, poster contests, and many other programs. At: http://www.rif.org

> **American Library Association** provides a number of reading initiatives, tons of booklists, and other information through its main website at http://www.ala.org and through its divisions: ALSC (Association for Library Services for Children), YALSA (Young Adult Library Services Association), and AASL (American Association of School Librarians).

Classroom Collections

Classroom collections have become quite popular in the last few years. The notion is that books and information should be at hand in addition to the repository down the hall in the library media center. Sometimes conflict develops over who owns what, inventory, and other matters. Resolution of such conflicts is not difficult when the larger vision of a school-wide print-rich environment is presented and implemented. In the age of technology, the conflict disappears as electronic sources go online.

Advantages of Print Classroom Collections	**Disadvantages of static (i.e. permanent) classroom collections**
➢ Print-rich = more reading ➢ Close at hand ➢ Close at hand ➢ Close at hand	➢ Interesting to students the first few weeks of school and not thereafter. ➢ Too small to have any significant variety. ➢ Cannot contain any in-depth information needed for research on various reading levels and in a variety of formats. ➢ Take up too much room as the collection grows. ➢ Another management problem for the teacher.

Solution: ROTATING Classroom Collections

➢ Working with the library media specialist, create rotating classroom collections using the LMC as the warehouse.
➢ The rotating collection should be as large as the classroom can handle.
➢ Some items might be semi-permanent, others rotating every few weeks.
➢ The collection would contain materials for free voluntary reading chosen by students.
➢ The collection would contain materials to be used in a curricular unit.
➢ Materials could be circulated from the classroom to the home.
➢ The collection would contain materials in many kinds of formats including books, paperbacks, magazines, newspapers, multimedia, etc.
➢ Every room collection would also contain electronic resources, databases, selected Internet sites, and other digital information and multimedia items flowing from the LMC into the classroom and into the home.
➢ The electronic classroom collection would contain links to the central LMC collection, local, district, and national resources.

Check out Jim Trealease's ideas for classroom display at:

http://www.trealease-on-reading.com/rah.chpt6_p4.htm/#rain-gutter

What about control? Loss? Repair? Replacement? Maintenance? Inventory? Funding? Ownership? Circulation from classrooms vs. circulation from the LMC?

Suggestion:
➢ Hold a brainstorming session with teachers.
➢ Decide first that literacy takes precedence (read some Krashen/McQuillan research together).
➢ Decide that physical print items <u>will</u> be everywhere and that the organization's needs are secondary to user's needs.
➢ Invent rules and procedures that will work for individuals (one size need not fit all).

Doing a Classroom Print-Rich Environment Audit

Idea: Once a month, do an audit of a single classroom or a grade-level or department classroom's print-rich environment. The classroom teacher and the library media specialist spend 20-30 minutes assessing the condition and status of the classroom collection then make decisions and future plans on this audit.

Genre Analysis
- Newspapers.
- Magazines.
- Novels representing a range of reading levels.
- Information books that answer and invite interesting questions.
- Books on tape (fiction and non-fiction).
- Poetry.
- Student writing.
- Picture books (regardless of student grade level).
- Speeches.
- Stories that connect to students' lives.
- Difficulty level. Span all needs?
- Interactive computer software.
- Links to online literature, writing, high-interest sites for reading.

Leadership Factors
- Involvement of parents.
- Budgeting.
- Part of school-wide reading initiative?
- Interface with the public library and other organizations.

Improvements and Solutions
- Things we can do instantly to improve the classroom collection.

- Things that will require setting up more formal plans and scheduling those actions.

- Things that will require administrative attention, long-term planning, budgeting, etc.

Facilities Analysis
- Space available – physical for books / computer connections for digital.
- Use of current space.
- Ideas for space reallocation.
- Display space.
- Shelving adequacy / needs.
- Use of boxes, bins, other containers.
- Space for student's books (personal, library media center checkouts, classroom materials).

Operations
- Condition of permanent collection.
- Condition of semi-permanent collection from the LMC.
- Check-out systems for student home use.
- System for rotating collections from the LMC – Who, when, how, what, how many?
- Status of temporary collections to match curricular studies.
- Involvement of students in maintaining classroom collections.
- Loss, replacement, repair.
- Sources for purchase / acquisition.
- Contents of collection (Of interest to students?)
- In-class promotion.
- Read-aloud, SSR time.
- Attractiveness of the collection and what to do about problems.
- Size of collection. Large enough?
- Use. Is it contributing to the amount each student reads?
- Student proposals to make it work better.
- Weeding as a part of the collection development plan.
- Book clubs and other classroom initiatives to build personal book ownership.
- Use and abuse of electronic reading initiatives.

Book Bags and Curiosity Kits:
An Idea for the Early Grades

Goal:		Result:
Each child from kindergarten through 2nd grade reads **500+** books per year.		Every reader will read at or above grade level and have a reading habit.

Try Book Bags. Each classroom acquires enough canvas book bags (either from commercial sources or by making them) for each child in the classroom, plus a few extras. Each book bag is numbered and can be decorated. Once a month, the class goes to the LMC, where the children help select the books for the book bags. Into each book bag goes a book that children can "read for themselves" (a wordless picture book, an alphabet book, books with a few words, highly illustrated books, etc.) and one book that can be read to the child by an older sibling, parent, friend, or caregiver (a good read-aloud picture book, a folktale, a nonfiction animal book, etc.). Back in the classroom, the book bags are hung on hooks or in cubbyholes. Each day as the children go home they take a different book bag, rotating throughout the month. The teacher keeps a list on a clipboard to record the book bag number next to the child's name. The homework for a kindergartner through second grader is to read two books a day. If the child forgets to bring the book bag back, the spares can be used. In no case is a child denied access to a book bag because reading practice is considered essential. The management of this program is considered a success when both the teacher and the library media specialist agree that the system requires very little monitoring. At the end of the month, the class revisits the LMC, where the books are exchanged for new ones. Books in the book bag program are checked out to the room. No individual circulation records are kept for these books.

Schools using this system report extremely low loss rates and damage, counting the cost of either as the cost of doing business. In addition to using the book bags, the class comes to the library once a month to choose books for the classroom collection (a minimum of 100 books at a time). And the students make other visits during the month to select their own personal books to take home in addition to the book bags. The typical kindergartener, first or second grader should have read a minimum of 500 books during the school year and then linked into the public library system for regular reading during vacation periods.

Curiosity Kits. A variant on the book bag program is the creation of curiosity kits where each child creates a book bag filled with 2+ books on a theme that they think other members of the class might be interested in: whales, riddles, drawing books, hobbies, paper airplanes, kite flying, etc.

Theme Bags: During a month when the teacher will be studying a topic, children fill a third or half the bags with books on the topic.

Parent Involvement Kits: Julie McFadden, Kindergarten Teacher at Fairmont Elementary School in New Albany, Indiana has a program where a bag containing a book with activities for the parent and child begs for parent involvement in literacy. It is worth writing for details (1725 Abbie Dell, New Albany IN 47150). A similar project know as "Literacy Backpacks for Kindergarteners" had high school students help in creating book-and –activity-filled backpacks for kindergartners to take home (Jo Anna Booher, Media Director, Northwest High School, 5525 W. 34th Street, Indianapolis IN 46224).

Electronic Reading Programs:
Opportunities and Challenges[1]

Electronic reading programs like Accelerated Reader and Reading Counts are relatively new tools becoming more widespread in the quest to create avid and capable readers. These programs vary greatly in cost and effectiveness, with Accelerated Reader (AR) leading the pack in popularity. The computer program awards points to readers based on taking tests. The tests provide feedback to learners and teachers and allow teachers to monitor the quantity and quality of reading learners do.

Before your school adopts Accelerated Reader or another electronic reading program, classroom teachers, administrators, and library media specialists might consider the potential uses and abuses:

Uses. When properly implemented, these programs can:

> ➢ Provide structure in building reading skills.
> ➢ Provide learners a mechanism for finding books at their own reading ability.
> ➢ Give learners instant feedback on their progress.
> ➢ Provide a way to track whether learners actually read and comprehend their books, and to encourage them to adjust their reading levels as appropriate.
> ➢ Help teachers identify at-risk children and help them get back on track quickly.
> ➢ Increase motivation and achievement (although the research is inconclusive on this point).
> ➢ Increase circulation from the library substantially.

Challenges - Potential Cautions. Some of the ways such a system can be abused include:

> ➢ Linking results to learners' grades. Studies have shown this has a negative effect on intrinsic motivation.
> ➢ Linking achievement to extrinsic rewards like food, toys, or play activities, or money. Such rewards may detract from the goal of fostering lifelong reading.
> ➢ Public posting of learners' results. While this may motivate high achievers, it can be disastrous for slow learners.
> ➢ Restricting curricular or library collection development based on what books are available within that reading program.
> ➢ Substituting the computer-based reading program assessments for reading activities that foster critical thinking. Most of these electronic reading programs test plot and factual knowledge rather than understanding.
> ➢ Library book budget spent mostly on books for this program.
> ➢ Adults who mistake an electronic reading program for a complete reading program.

Suggested Fixes. (since machines should never get in the way of literacy):

> ➢ Any book a learner wants to read should be a "program" book. "Extra credit" points can be assigned during a reading conference/discussion by the teacher, library media specialist, or volunteer adult.
> ➢ If a young person wants to read something for which there is no test, have that child develop the test for points. Whether the test actually gets on to the computer is a matter of time and manpower.
> ➢ While most of what is read might be "at grade level," children should be allowed, even encouraged, to stretch and read anything they are motivated to read.

---

[1] Helpful articles about AR include: Topping, Keith. "Formative Assessment of Reading Comprehension by Computer." *Reading Online*, posted November, 1999. Available at: (http://www.readingonline.org/critical/topping/index.html) and Labbo, Linda. "Questions Worth Asking About the Accelerated Reader: A Response to Topping." *Reading Online*, posted November, 1999. Available at: (http://www.readingonline.org/critical/labbo/index.html) Also: Chenoweth, Karin. "Keeping Score," *School Library Journal*, September, 2001, pp. 48-51.

Supporting Reading in the School

Regardless of the experience of classroom teachers or library media specialists, there are two strategies that can improve both performance and attitudes toward reading.

Start SSR (sustained silent reading)

As learners progress through school, they spend less and less time reading independently during class. However, many learners do not make up for this by increased time reading independently at home. SSR (sustained silent reading) is a response to this reality that holds myriad benefits.

Ten Reasons to Start SSR Today:
1. Increases the amount students read. Amount counts.
2. Builds vocabulary through exposure to words in context.
3. Offers learners an opportunity to read materials of their own choice.
4. Leads to more reading outside of school.
5. Provides on-going opportunities for adults to model reading behavior with students.
6. Increases fluency in second language learners.
7. Helps develop reading as a habit.
8. Broadens and deepens students' knowledge base.
9. Places value on reading for pleasure.
10. Fosters a love of reading and a love of learning.

Read Aloud

Some teachers and administrators feel reading aloud is a poor use of instructional time, particularly at the secondary level. In fact, reading aloud is so effective it should be done every day in classes K-12.

Benefits of Reading Aloud to Learners:
➢ Builds vocabulary and background knowledge.
➢ Establishes the reading-writing connection.
➢ Introduces the nuances of language.
➢ Helps promote a love of reading.
➢ Helps introduce types of reading students may not discover independently.
➢ Provides risk-free opportunities for students to enjoy the richness of written language.

Library Media Specialists Help Teachers Read Aloud By:
➢ Locating high interest literature selections for the teacher.
➢ Reinforcing good modeling by reading aloud to students during booktalks, promotions, and other library visits.
➢ Locating selections relevant to the classroom teacher's specific curriculum.

"The single most important activity for building the knowledge required for eventual success in reading is reading aloud to students."[1]

---

[1] Anderson, Richard C. and Elfrieda Hiebert, et al. *Becoming a Nation of Readers: The Report of the Commission on Reading.* Washington, DC: National Institute of Education, 1985.

Indiana Student Publishing Ideas

Encouraging learners to publish their own writing whether on the web or in print format provides many benefits. One such example is the *Tales by the Schoolside* book published by the staff and students of Sarah Scott Middle School in Vigo County Indiana. Every teacher and administrator of the school paired with a learner to produce a collection of original writings illustrated by student artists. The resulting book made this a memorable learning experience and a family keepsake. Here are a few tips for creating such a program.

Getting Started

➤ "Empowering Student Learning with Web Publishing" by Tammy Payton includes information on how to get started, links to AUPs for elementary and secondary, links to student writing, web page evaluation and more. At: http://www. siec.k12.in.us/~west/article/ publish.htm

➤ Loogootee Community Schools in Loogootee Indiana – "Permission to Publish Student Work" form. At: http://www.siec.k12.in.us/~west/article/ permission.htm

➤ **Connected Classroom** web site on student publishing provides links to evaluation rubrics and examples of student writing. At: http://www.

Examples of Indiana Student Writing Published Online

➤ Online activities developed by 1st and 2nd graders at Loogootee Elementary. Reindeer. At: http://www.siec.k12. in.us/~west/proj/claus/intro.htm

➤ Clark Elementary School 2nd graders in Whiteland Indiana Adjectives. At: http://homepage.mac.com/gwagoner2 31/grade2/adjectiveartlist.html

➤ Students, ages 8-12, in Mrs. Joan Globe's Media Club interviewed Cannelton residents and created "Echoes of Cannelton" to preserve the town's history. At: www.siec.k12.in.us/cannelton/ echoes/narritive.htm

Places Students Can Publish

➤ **Kids Bookshelf** - Publishes student stories, poems and book reviews. At: http://www.kidsbookshelf. com/index.asp

➤ **Kids'Space** – A place kids can share stories, pictures and music online. At: http://www.kids-space.org/navi/about.html

➤ **MidLink Magazine** - The Digital Magazine by Students, for Students - Ages 8 – 18. At: http://longwood.cs.ucf.edu/~MidLink/

➤ **Publishing Student Work On-line** - A collection of web sites containing student work online. At: http://k12science.ati.stevens-tech.edu/tutorials/studentpub/resources.htm

➤ **Scholastic's Writing With Writers** - Online workshops for students, with various writers. At: http://teacher.scholastic.com/writewit/index.htm

➤ **Stone Soup Magazine.** At: http://www.stonesoup.com/

➤ **The Young Writers' Club** - An on-line club that aims to encourage children of all ages to enjoy writing as a creative pastime by getting them to share their work and help each other improve their writing abilities. At: http://www.cs.bilkent.edu.tr/~david/derya/ywc.html

Idea: Make the library media center the place to store learner-written books for circulation, a digitization center for archival storage, and the central index of digital work with full-text access.

Reading Beyond the Textbook

Learners can read far beyond the few paragraphs in the textbook to find both interesting and fascinating ideas connected with any curricular subject. Such reading, whether in books, magazines, or on the Internet will contribute to reading competence as well as content knowledge. Here are just a few reading extension ideas.

Sorting the World of Opinion
On any issue, have groups read various articles (think Inspire) and create an opinion timeline placing ideas along an opinion spectrum. Have each article read by two independent groups or individuals who must agree on its placement on the opinion spectrum. (pro-war vs. anti-war; for and against environmental issues; etc.)

Connections to History:
Link learners to Indiana historical documents making a collage of historical events with evidence from real documents of the event. What are the difference between what real documents say and how historians view the event? (Use Inspire as a source)

Building Background Knowledge
Combine a read-aloud (teacher reads a book starting a week or so before the unit begins) with a library media center visit to just "read the pictures" in books dealing with the unit topic, or to have the learners preview possible videos/multi-media web sites to show to the whole class, or a library media center visit to have the class discover a relevant room collection for the unit topic.

Hall of Fame
Have learners contribute to a giant collage of people of a time or contrasting people by collecting and reading facts, experiences of the person, writing excerpts from the person's works and then comparing all these sources with any short encyclopedia articles or textbook "briefs" to judge whether encyclopedists are "fair" and accurate.

Another Point of View:
Students read articles, books, or web pages offering an alternative view to the accepted version of the topic you're studying. Students look for reasons the alternative view is not more widely accepted or explain the faulty reasoning for the alternative view.

Poetry, Short Stories, Drama, Novels:
Students read fiction about the topic and write their own fiction in a similar style.

Extending the Lesson
Encourage students showing a keen interest in a topic to read about it more extensively. Work with teachers to provide interesting and high quality trade books or articles on the topic.

Have a Special Theme SSR Time
Help assemble a temporary classroom collection on the theme for SSR time during a unit.

Focusing the Library Media Program to Achieve Targets Both State and Federal

The federal government has targeted five areas in the "No Child Left Behind Act" initiative as the essential components of reading instruction. (At: http://www.ed.gov/offices/OESE/readingfirst/) They are:

1. **Phonemic Awareness -** The ability to hear, identify and manipulate the individual sounds – phonemes – in spoken words. Phonemic awareness is the understanding that the sounds of spoken language work together to make words.

2. **Phonics** – The understanding that there is a predictable relationship between phonemes – the sounds of spoken language – the graphemes – the letters and spellings that represent those sounds in written language. Readers use these relationships to recognize familiar words accurately and automatically and to decode unfamiliar words.

3. **Vocabulary Development** – Development of stored information about the meanings and pronunciation of words necessary for communication: listening, speaking, reading, and writing vocabulary.

4. **Reading fluency, including oral reading skills** – Fluency is the ability to read text accurately and quickly. It provides a bridge between word recognition and comprehension. Fluent readers recognize words and comprehend at the same time.

5. **Reading comprehension strategies** – strategies for understanding, remembering, and communicating with others about what has been read. Comprehension strategies are sets of steps that purposeful, active readers use to make sense of text.

[Indiana's additional target:]

6. **Reading Motivation**

The Reading First initiative in Indiana targets federal funding toward the five essential reading components and requires that individual sites promote projects based on scientifically based reading research. **While reading motivation is not one of the components, it can be used to stimulate the skills listed.** What can library media center and technology programs do to build the skills list?

Sample Support and Interventions:	Library Media Specialists and Technology Specialists Can:
Instructional Materials - Selection and implementation of instructional materials, including educational technology such as software and other digital curricula, that are based on scientifically based reading research.	Assist in the selection of texts, computer programs and supplementary materials to support the program.
Access to Reading Materials – Promotion of reading and library programs that provide access to engaging reading material.	Provide both the materials and the access in large enough quantities to make a difference.[1]
Development of Vocabulary and Comprehension	Concentrate on the "amount" read by every child.[2]

---

[1] The Lance studies (see page 13) reported the difference large school library collections had on reading.

[2] Many studies link the amount read to vocabulary and comprehension growth. (See p. 57)

Checklist on Support of Reading From the Library Media Program

How does your school library media program support reading? A checklist:

Access:
- ❑ Does the budget allow for the purchase of at least two books per year per child?
- ❑ Do students have flexible access to the books and other reading materials in the school library?
- ❑ Does the circulation policy encourage students to take home unlimited numbers of reading materials?
- ❑ Are the classrooms regularly supplied with new collections of reading materials from the school library?
- ❑ Are paperback books available in book bags, baskets, and other containers in the lunchroom and other areas throughout the school?

Strategies
- ❑ Is a sustained silent reading or similar program in place in the school?
- ❑ Are students read to daily for 15 minutes or more?
- ❑ Do teachers and the media specialist convey the message that free voluntary reading is a priority?
- ❑ Do the school and public library work together to promote reading?
- ❑ Do students have the opportunity to participate in the Young Hoosier Book Award, Read Across America, and other activities that promote reading?
- ❑ Are booktalks by teachers, media specialists and students given on a regular basis?
- ❑ Are students involved in choral reading, puppetry and readers' theater?

Collections
- ❑ Does the school library have a large selection of high interest, appealing reading materials that students will enjoy?
- ❑ Is there a large budget to refresh the collection each year to keep it of interest to readers?
- ❑ Are books available to support units of study that are attractive, well-illustrated and at appropriate reading levels?
- ❑ Is there a collection of videotapes and CD-ROMs that support reading for pleasure and information?
- ❑ Do students have the opportunity to suggest or select new titles for the collection?

Linking English/Language Arts Standards and Library Media Center Reading Programs

Many states have set out academic standards for the teaching or the language arts. These standards often do not mention the word "library." One presumes a strong library media program if the standards are to be implemented effectively. Together, library media specialists and teachers develop plans to strengthen the language arts program at all ability and grade levels.

➢ **Idea:** Hold a Language Arts Summit

➢ **Who:** Principal, reading specialists, teachers, library media specialists, community representatives, other guests as invited.

➢ **Engaging Problem:** How can the library media center and the language arts program complement each other to create a school-wide community of readers?

➢ **Worksheet:**

List of Major Language Arts Standards and Elements	How the Library Media Program Can Respond

List of the Major Library Media Center Reading Program Elements	How the Language Arts Program/Teachers Can Respond

➢ **Task:** Create a collaborative and integrated language arts/library media center program plan.

➢ **Resources:** What do we already have? What do we need? How will we get what we need?

Could print p. 73 on the back of this sheet.

Starter Sample of LMC/Language Arts Program Links

List of Major Language Arts Standards and Elements	**How the Library Media Program Can Respond**
Phonemic Awareness (1st grade): Students understand the basic features of words. They see letter patterns and know how to translate them into spoken language by using phonics. They apply this knowledge to achieve fluent (smooth and clear) oral and silent reading.	➢ In storytelling, reading aloud, the library media specialist selects stories where word sounds are a natural part of the whole. ➢ Word and letter sounds are a fun part of storytime. ➢ The library media specialist furnishes an ample supply of books where word sounds are a natural part of the literature. ➢ Parent program exists to help on letter sounds.
Comprehension and Analysis of Grade-Level-Appropriate Text (8th grade): Students read and understand grade-level-appropriate material. They describe and connect the essential ideas, arguments, and perspectives of the text by using their knowledge of text structure, organization, and purpose…	➢ The library media specialist arranges for online databases and selected web sites to provide students the variety of information they need that matches their level. ➢ The library media specialist teaches text structure as students encounter a variety of information sources. ➢ The teacher and the library media specialist team as the learners interact with the information.

List of the Major Library Media Center Reading Program Elements	**How the Language Arts Program/Teachers Can Respond**
➢ The library media specialist notices that in social studies, many learners cannot understand the chapters in the textbook because they are too difficult or the learners do not speak English very well. The library contains a plethora of materials on the topic at hand.	➢ The teacher and the library media specialist work together to choose reading materials on many levels and provide the learners with a wide choice in what they should read on the topic. ➢ Discussion and other activities done by the teacher and library media specialist insure that every learner has a deep understanding of the content knowledge.
➢ The library media specialist has acquired site licenses for word processing and outlining software to help learners both organize their thoughts and make the writing process more efficient.	➢ The teacher and the library media specialist team to teach the new tools including data collection and organization when a major writing project is due.

Note: Sample standards on this page come from Indiana Language Arts Standards. If teachers in Indiana schools are using the Four Blocks program at: http://davidstoner.org/4blocks/ they will be dividing their language arts instructional time into a reading block, a words block, a choice reading block, and a writing block. Library media specialists can use those state guidelines to find areas for collaboration, particularly in the choice reading block where students are encouraged to read widely.

Reading:
Professional Development Opportunities

➤ **Association for Media Educators (AIME)** sponsors an annual conference in the fall featuring children's book authors, workshops and exhibits of new books. At: http://www.ilfonline.org/Conf/AIME%20Conf/index.htm

➤ **The Buddy Teaching and Learning Center** (BTLC), a professional development center, offers free or almost free one, two and three day workshops for Indiana educators. Examples with a reading focus include: Where the Rubber Meets the Road: Standards-based Language Arts Activities and Ideas (Grades K-5, Writing with Technology Tools, Little Kids Can Too!; Integrating Writing and Technology. At: http://www.btlc.org

➤ **Children's Literature Conference, Butler University, Indianapolis, is** held on the last Saturday of January yearly. Award-winning children's books authors and illustrators are featured along with workshops on children's literature. Contact: Children's Literature Conference, Butler University, 4600 Sunset Avenue, Indianapolis, IN, 46208

➤ **Children & Young People's Division** of the IN Library Federation sponsors a conference each fall featuring workshops about books, reading, authors, illustrators and programs. At: http://www.ilfonline.org/Conf/CYPD/cypdconf.htm

➤ **Four Blocks** (Gr 1-2), **Big Blocks** (Gr 4-6) and other reading workshops are offered by the Educational Service Centers across the state. Check for specific information at the service center in your area. At: http://doe.state.in.us/esc/welcome.html

➤ **Indiana State Reading Association** sponsors state programs, conferences and meetings planned to provide knowledge that will assist educators to solve reading problems and stimulate the love of reading as a lifelong habit. Contact: Scott Popplewell, Executive Director, Ball State Teacher's College 311, Muncie, IN 47306: (765) 285-8560 (email: spopplew@bsu.edu) At: www.indianareads.org/mission.htm

➤ **IN Writing Initiative** - The Indiana Writing Development Project is a statewide initiative developed in partnership with the Indiana Department of Education (IDOE) and the Indiana Education Service Centers for teachers to gain confidence in their ability to teach the writing process. An ongoing series of five days of writing development training are held at sites in the northern, central, and southern areas of the state. At: http://davidstoner.org/irwin/

➤ **Indiana Writing Project** sponsors a summer institute at Ball State for teachers with 3+ yrs experience. Participants write, research topics in the teaching of writing, and present to each other successful, practical teaching techniques. At: http://www.bsu.edu/english/events/iwp/home.htm

➤ **International Reading Association** – Their annual Convention is held each spring to give professionals a chance to exchange information with peers, gain access to resources, and network with other professionals. For information on the national, state and regional conferences. At: http://www.reading.org/meetings/conv/

➤ **IREAD:** Indiana's Reading Excellence Action Demonstration Program. This federal grant, for improving literacy in Indiana's K-3 high poverty/low achievement schools, provides professional development resources. At: http://doe.state.in.us/rea/profdev.html

Assessment of the LMC Impact on Reading

Both learners and teachers are often quite willing to invest time and effort to integrate technology when it is accessible and it works. Collecting, reviewing, and reporting data at the organizational level, the teaching unit level and the learner level will help assess the impact technology is ready to make and is making in the school.

Level of Measure	Factor	Sources of Data
LMC Reading at the Organization Level (District and School)	The state of the support of both the LMC reading program and the reading curriculum.	❑ Number and percent of learners participating successfully in school-wide reading initiatives. ❑ Number and percent of readers who participate in SSR time. ❑ The number and percent of readers on or above grade level on reading scores. ❑ The annual budget for reading materials for the LMC reading program meets the needs of the school. ❑ The number and percent of teachers reading aloud every day to learners.
LMC Reading at the Learning Unit Level (class interaction and use)	The impact the LMC reading program has on classrooms print-rich environments, the language arts curriculum, and units of instruction where reading can be integrated.	❑ The number by discipline or grade level of collaborative units where a "reading" component is present. ❑ The extent to which both fiction and nonfiction was integrated into collaborative units. ❑ Evidence that the LMC reading program and the language arts goals were integrated in a collaborative unit. ❑ The number of classrooms that have rotating classroom collections from the LMC.
LMC Reading at the Learner Level (as individuals)	Individual progress by each learner as a capable and avid reader.	❑ The reading scores of an individual student. (see note 1 below) ❑ Evidence of individual progress in reading from measures other than state or standardized tests. ❑ Evidence from an attitudinal measure that the learner is both an avid and capable reader. ❑ Reading log analysis (including amount read). ❑ Points from electronic reading programs ❑ Scores on writing assessments (see Note 2 below) ❑ Score on Cornwell's Independent Reading Rubric (see p.76)

Note 1: The federal No Child Left Behind Act and the funding through ESEA requires states and schools that qualify for federal money to use "scientifically based" research to systematically and empirically use methods that draw on observation or experimentation. "For reporting purposes, the federal government is requiring that evidence be collected on the number and percentage of K-3 students who are reading at or above grade level. States must also include data on the academic status of subgroups of students who are traditionally "left behind" – students who are economically disadvantaged, come from minority groups, have disabilities, or have limited English proficiency"[1] In the real world of schools, as long as the federal data is collected as required, many other techniques and data collection techniques are acceptable. For opposing views to the federal program, read Allington"s *Big Brother and the Educational Reading Curriculum.*[2]

Note 2: The Indiana Writing Development Project has developed guidelines for assessing written products using dichotomous and analytic scales, primary trait scoring, feature analysis, and atomistic assessment. These techniques can be seen at http://davidstoner.org/twin/evaluation.htm

---

[1] "Reading's New Rules: ESEA Demands a Scientific Approach," *Education Update*, August 2002, p. 5

[2] Allington, Richard L. *Big Brother and the National Reading Curriculum: How Ideology Trumped Evidence.* Portsmouth, NH: Heinemann, 2002.

Independent Reading Rubric
A Learner Level Assessment

By Linda L. Cornwell[1]

An essential key to becoming a proficient reader is independent reading practice. Research suggests that it is the volume of reading that students do that enhances their reading achievement. The following rubric is divided into four major categories: materials selection, reading behaviors, engagement/attitudes, and accountability.

MATERIALS SELECTION

Developing	Progressing	Proficient
• Rarely selects materials at his or her independent reading level.	• Frequently selects materials at his or her independent reading level.	• Consistently selects materials at his or her independent reading level.
• Limits reading choices to a narrow range of topics or a single genre.	• Reads beyond favorite topics, genres, and authors.	• Reads a wide variety of genres, authors, and topics.
• Often has difficulty in selecting appropriate independent reading materials without assistance.	• Occasionally needs assistance in finding appropriate independent reading materials.	• Finds appropriate independent reading materials without assistance.

ENGAGEMENT/ATTITUDES

Developing	Progressing	Proficient
• Often complains about reading and fails to exhibit pleasure in independent reading.	• Generally exhibits a positive attitude toward independent reading.	• Frequently expresses pleasure regarding independent reading.
• Does not exhibit confidence as a reader.	• Generally exhibits confidence as a reader.	• Consistently exhibits confidence as a reader and sees himself/herself as a reader.
• Fails to set reading goals and reads a minimal amount during the allotted time.	• Sets realistic reading goals and usually achieves those goals during the allotted time.	• Sets high reading goals and reads the maximum amount during the allotted time.
• Rarely finishes the material chosen for independent reading.	• Finishes most selections chosen for independent reading.	• Rarely abandons an independent reading selection before finishing it.

READING BEHAVIORS

Developing	Progressing	Proficient
• Seldom has material available and ready to read.	• Generally has material available and ready to read.	• Consistently has material available and ready to read.
• Is unable to sustain focus or read without interruption for the allotted time.	• Usually sustains focus and reads without interruption for the allotted time.	• Reads continuously without interruption for the allotted time.
• Continuously seeks peer or teacher assistance in reading the material.	• Self-corrects before seeking peer or teacher assistance and requires a minimum amount of help from others in reading the material.	• Rarely requires peer or teacher assistance in reading the material.
• Uses reading time inappropriately: disrupts others, daydreams, doodles, wanders about the room, doesn't read, etc.	• Generally uses reading time appropriately.	• Consistently uses reading time appropriately.

ACCOUNTABILITY

Developing	Progressing	Proficient
• Rarely completes the reading log after independent reading.	• Generally completes the reading log after independent reading.	• Consistently and accurately completes the reading log after independent reading.
• Rarely reflects upon and/or shares thoughts about what he or she has read.	• Generally reflects upon and shares thoughts about what he or she has read.	• Consistently reflects upon, shares thoughts about what he or she has read and makes connections to self and others.
• Rarely recommends reading materials to others.	• Frequently recommends reading materials to others when asked.	• Voluntarily and continuously recommends reading materials to others.

---

[1] Originally printed in *NetWords*, Spring, 2002, p. 7 (Middle Grades Reading Network); revised by the author, Oct., 2002.

ENHANCING LEARNING THROUGH TECHNOLOGY

 **Technology**

So much money, so much time, and so much effort has been made to equip the nation's school with technology, yet so many questions remain. Never has a tool of change come to education with higher expectations.

Charged with the responsibility of providing a high-tech and information-rich environment for the school, technology specialists and library media specialists must address a wide variety of expectations for technology. Consider those of two major national documents:

Expectations for Students	Expectations for Organizations
NCREL's Phases of Technology Use for Students	**The enGauge Essential Conditions for Use of Technology to Prepare Students to Learn, Work, and Live Successfully…**

Expectations for Students

NCREL's Phases of Technology Use for Students

Phase 1: Print Automation – technology automates print-based practices with some increase in active hands-on learning.
Phase II: Expansion of Learning Opportunities - Students use technology to organize and produce reports, often using multimedia formats.
Phase III: Data-Driven Virtual Learning - Students use technology to explore diverse information resources inside and outside school and produce information for real-world tasks.

Source: NCREL: Phases of Computer-Based Learning at: http://www.ncrel.org/tplan/cbtl/phases.htm

Expectations for Organizations

The enGauge Essential Conditions for Use of Technology to Prepare Students to Learn, Work, and Live Successfully…

Forward-Thinking, Shared Vision
Effective Teaching and Learning Practices
Educator Proficiency With Effective Teaching and Learning Practices
Digital-Age Equity
Robust Access Anywhere, Anytime
Systems and Leadership

Source: NCREL's enGauge web site at: http://www.ncrel.org/engauge/framewk/sitemap.htm

The purpose of the technology section of this book is to help answer the question:

Are we making any progress?

Focusing Technology on the Learner[1]

In the past twenty years as a technology-rich environment has developed in education, local, state, and national documents are very clear that the focus of the investment in technology must be upon the learner. Compare the vision of major documents to your own local vision.

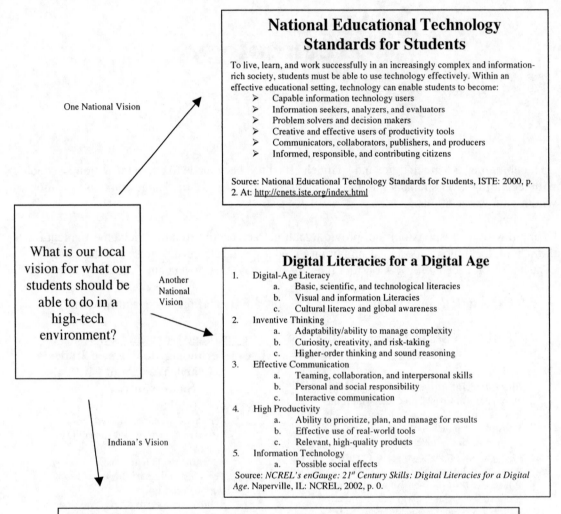

One National Vision

National Educational Technology Standards for Students

To live, learn, and work successfully in an increasingly complex and information-rich society, students must be able to use technology effectively. Within an effective educational setting, technology can enable students to become:

➢ Capable information technology users
➢ Information seekers, analyzers, and evaluators
➢ Problem solvers and decision makers
➢ Creative and effective users of productivity tools
➢ Communicators, collaborators, publishers, and producers
➢ Informed, responsible, and contributing citizens

Source: National Educational Technology Standards for Students, ISTE: 2000, p. 2. At: http://cnets.iste.org/index.html

What is our local vision for what our students should be able to do in a high-tech environment?

Another National Vision

Digital Literacies for a Digital Age

1. Digital-Age Literacy
   a. Basic, scientific, and technological literacies
   b. Visual and information Literacies
   c. Cultural literacy and global awareness
2. Inventive Thinking
   a. Adaptability/ability to manage complexity
   b. Curiosity, creativity, and risk-taking
   c. Higher-order thinking and sound reasoning
3. Effective Communication
   a. Teaming, collaboration, and interpersonal skills
   b. Personal and social responsibility
   c. Interactive communication
4. High Productivity
   a. Ability to prioritize, plan, and manage for results
   b. Effective use of real-world tools
   c. Relevant, high-quality products
5. Information Technology
   a. Possible social effects

Source: *NCREL's enGauge: 21ˢᵗ Century Skills: Digital Literacies for a Digital Age.* Naperville, IL: NCREL, 2002, p. 0.

Indiana's Vision

"Communities of learners are engaged in lifelong learning and are contributing members of the global and digital information world – learners who have problem-solving and higher-order critical thinking skills, information and communication skills, access to current and real-world information and tools, and mastery of core basic skills."
Source: *Indiana's K-12 Plan for Technology.* At: http://www.doe.state.in.us/olr/pdf/strategicplan.pdf

The Bottom Line: Technology is not an add-on in Indiana schools. Technology and information literacy are embedded in the Indiana Academic Standards.

---

[1] For a documented vision of what exemplary high-tech school experiences look like, read: The George Lucas Educational Foundation. *Edutopia: Success Stories for Learning in the Digital Age.* San Francisco, CA: Jossey-Bass, 2002.

Empowering Teachers with Technology

Both the technology specialist and the library media specialist have the responsibility to see that teachers are comfortable and knowledgeable using the local technological environment. National and state documents are very helpful in making local plans.

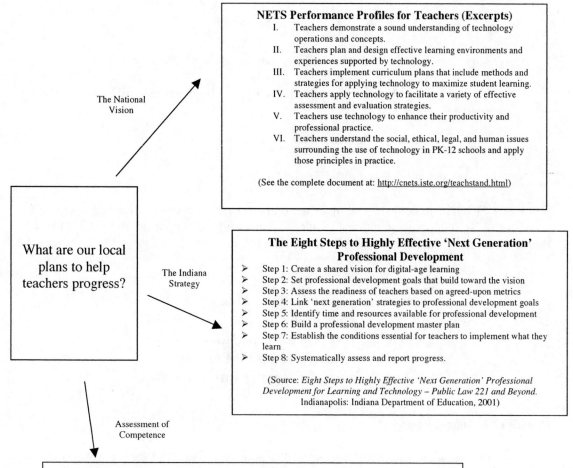

The National Vision

NETS Performance Profiles for Teachers (Excerpts)
I. Teachers demonstrate a sound understanding of technology operations and concepts.
II. Teachers plan and design effective learning environments and experiences supported by technology.
III. Teachers implement curriculum plans that include methods and strategies for applying technology to maximize student learning.
IV. Teachers apply technology to facilitate a variety of effective assessment and evaluation strategies.
V. Teachers use technology to enhance their productivity and professional practice.
VI. Teachers understand the social, ethical, legal, and human issues surrounding the use of technology in PK-12 schools and apply those principles in practice.

(See the complete document at: http://cnets.iste.org/teachstand.html)

What are our local plans to help teachers progress?

The Indiana Strategy

The Eight Steps to Highly Effective 'Next Generation' Professional Development
➢ Step 1: Create a shared vision for digital-age learning
➢ Step 2: Set professional development goals that build toward the vision
➢ Step 3: Assess the readiness of teachers based on agreed-upon metrics
➢ Step 4: Link 'next generation' strategies to professional development goals
➢ Step 5: Identify time and resources available for professional development
➢ Step 6: Build a professional development master plan
➢ Step 7: Establish the conditions essential for teachers to implement what they learn
➢ Step 8: Systematically assess and report progress.

(Source: *Eight Steps to Highly Effective 'Next Generation' Professional Development for Learning and Technology – Public Law 221 and Beyond.* Indianapolis: Indiana Department of Education, 2001)

Assessment of Competence

➢ *My Target:* This assessment tool includes a framework of technology skills and competencies for teachers, administrators, and trainers. At: http://mytarget. iassessment.org/tool.html.

➢ *Learning with Technology Toolkit:* An assessment tool designed to help educators assess the use of technology in their own practice. Download this tool at: http://ncrtec.org/capacity/profile/profile.htm

➢ *enGauge Online Assessment:* allows a district or school to conduct online assessment of school or system-wide educational technology effectiveness. At: http://www.ncrel.org/engauge/assess/assess.htm

The Technology Climate:
Everyone a Skilled User of Technology

In a sea of technological devices, upgrades, and new software versions, the list of skills everyone needs has grown exponentially:

➤ Equipment operation and care

➤ Software and materials care

➤ Word processing, database construction, and spreadsheets

➤ Layout and graphic design for presentations and communication in print, video, and multimedia formats

➤ Internet and information system searching and use

New versions and upgrades of software and hardware

Few if any can claim expertise on all machines and information systems. Likewise, keeping a wide array of technologies operational requires a community of supportive and helpful users. Hence the critical compact between adults and learners:

You Teach Me
I Teach You
We Teach Each Other
We All Help Keep It Working
In a Safe and Nurturing Environment

Questions for our school:

1. Are the computers in classrooms up to date and hooked into the library media center network?
2. Can teachers take their whole class, individuals, or small groups to a location where there are reliable computers hooked into the library media center network?
3. Is there a wireless network and bank of computers that can be sent to any location when learners need a computer for an assignment?
4. Do the professional and technical staff of the school provide "just-in-time" instruction in either software or hardware operation as needed?
5. Have we designated various learners to be "coaches" as we proceed into a computer assignment?
6. Do we talk often about the "helping" atmosphere as we all use the high-tech networks?
7. Do we talk about ethical use of information?
8. Do we have rules and help each other avoid potentially dangerous problems in the Internet world?

Knowledge of Technology Systems

Not all technology specialists or library media specialists have the expertise to build the technology infrastructure of the school and district, yet some knowledge of the infrastructure is essential if meaningful conversations and educational designs for networks and other matters are to take place. Consider the following list of factors that constitute the technology infrastructure.

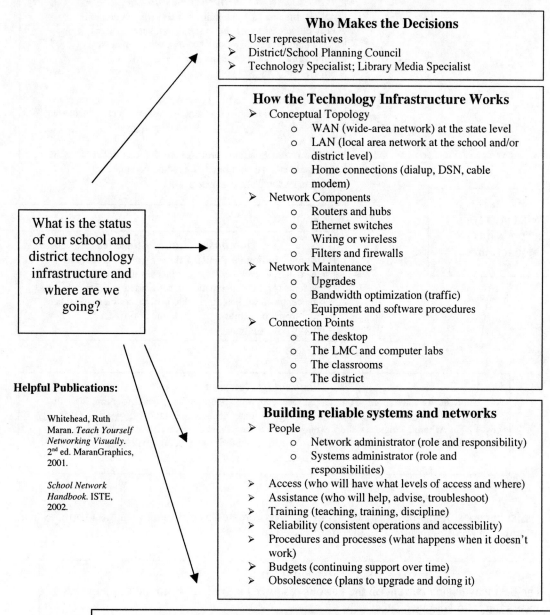

What is the status of our school and district technology infrastructure and where are we going?

Who Makes the Decisions
- ➤ User representatives
- ➤ District/School Planning Council
- ➤ Technology Specialist; Library Media Specialist

How the Technology Infrastructure Works
- ➤ Conceptual Topology
    - o WAN (wide-area network) at the state level
    - o LAN (local area network at the school and/or district level)
    - o Home connections (dialup, DSN, cable modem)
- ➤ Network Components
    - o Routers and hubs
    - o Ethernet switches
    - o Wiring or wireless
    - o Filters and firewalls
- ➤ Network Maintenance
    - o Upgrades
    - o Bandwidth optimization (traffic)
    - o Equipment and software procedures
- ➤ Connection Points
    - o The desktop
    - o The LMC and computer labs
    - o The classrooms
    - o The district

Helpful Publications:

Whitehead, Ruth Maran. *Teach Yourself Networking Visually.* 2nd ed. MaranGraphics, 2001.

School Network Handbook. ISTE, 2002.

Building reliable systems and networks
- ➤ People
    - o Network administrator (role and responsibility)
    - o Systems administrator (role and responsibilities)
- ➤ Access (who will have what levels of access and where)
- ➤ Assistance (who will help, advise, troubleshoot)
- ➤ Training (teaching, training, discipline)
- ➤ Reliability (consistent operations and accessibility)
- ➤ Procedures and processes (what happens when it doesn't work)
- ➤ Budgets (continuing support over time)
- ➤ Obsolescence (plans to upgrade and doing it)

Helpful Organizations
- ➤ **ICE** (Indiana Computer Educators) assists the educators of Indiana through the use of technology. At: http://www.iupui.edu/~ice/
- ➤ **HECC** (Hoosier Educational Computer Coordinators) focuses on issues of importance to leaders of technology coordination/administration. At: http://www.hecc.k12.in.us/

Utilizing the Best Indiana Technology Resources

Indiana has invested heavily in the creation of a wide variety of resources available to provide content via technology for teachers and learners. Knowing what is available, keeping up, linking to, and providing feedback on effectiveness to the state is a part of every technology leader's role.

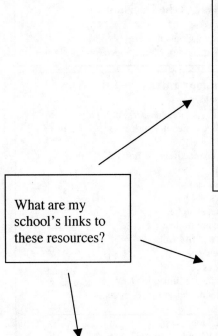

Internet Resources **ASAP** (Indiana Accountability System for Academic Progress) – Provides access to academic standards, best practices, accountability, professional develop, school data, school improvement plans, state aims and goals. At: http://ideanet.doe.state.in.us/asap. **Lesson Locator** (a section of **ASAP**) Provides standardized lesson plans for Indiana teachers. Access by level, subject area, and standard. At: http://www.lessonlocator.org/ **Indiana Web Academy** provides web-based resources for the entire educational community including parents. At: http://www.indianawebacademy.org.

What are my school's links to these resources?

Databases/Digital Libraries **Inspire – Indiana's Virtual Library** – offers electronic magazines, encyclopedias, and other resources to all Indiana residents for their information needs. Research, current events, science, business, health, notable people, hobbies, and much more from your library, school, home or office. At: http://www.inspire.net

Video and Television ❑ **Cable in the Classroom:** Commercial-free, copyright-cleared educational programming with accompanying academic standard-based support materials available at: **http://www.incable.org/** ❑ **Vision Athena:** Programs, short events, mini-courses, interactive or virtual field trips – all available to a school equipped with two-way distance-learning technology. Homepage and searchable catalog available at: http://www.visionathena.k12.in.us/va/content/events/search.asp.

To assist in choosing the best resources, enGauge has created a resource evaluation form. See at: http://www.ncrel.org/engauge/resource/toolform.htm.

Keeping Up The best way to stay current on the various resources in Indiana from the state level is to access the following web sites: ❑ Indiana Department of Public Instruction (http://www.doe.state.in.us/olr ❑ This book's website: http://www.indianalearns.org

Technology in Times of Scarce Resources

Times of economic downturn are cyclical reminders that belt tightening is the order of the day. Making "lemons out of lemonade" strategies may stimulate us to slow down, re-assess, and rethink in a high-tech world that seems to spin faster and faster. Here are a few ideas that might be considered.

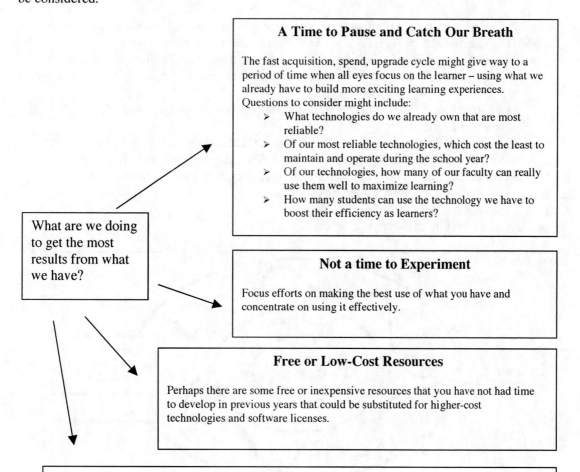

What are we doing to get the most results from what we have?

A Time to Pause and Catch Our Breath

The fast acquisition, spend, upgrade cycle might give way to a period of time when all eyes focus on the learner – using what we already have to build more exciting learning experiences. Questions to consider might include:

- ➢ What technologies do we already own that are most reliable?
- ➢ Of our most reliable technologies, which cost the least to maintain and operate during the school year?
- ➢ Of our technologies, how many of our faculty can really use them well to maximize learning?
- ➢ How many students can use the technology we have to boost their efficiency as learners?

Not a time to Experiment

Focus efforts on making the best use of what you have and concentrate on using it effectively.

Free or Low-Cost Resources

Perhaps there are some free or inexpensive resources that you have not had time to develop in previous years that could be substituted for higher-cost technologies and software licenses.

Cooperating with Others

- ➢ Indiana Education Service Centers (nine regions) were formed to stimulate collaborative efforts focusing on innovative student programs, professional development, advanced technological resources, and cooperative purchasing. Perhaps a second look at their services and a conversation with their staff might produce some new directions in cooperation. At: http://doe.state.in.us/esc
- ➢ Federal, state, and local governmental agencies might have untapped resources that have been overlooked.
- ➢ The local business community might be tapped for expertise as much as for funding.
- ➢ INCOLSA, Indiana's statewide library network, provides reference, interlibrary loan, training and continuing education, INSPIRE, technology support, and other services at: http://www.incolsa.net/

Resource: *Beyond Hardware – Using Existing Technology to Promote Higher-Level Thinking.* Eugene, OR: ISTE, 2002. Provides ideas for educators for promoting higher-order thinking skills with limited technology.

Times of downturn might be the best times to plan and to strengthen our political clout.

Building the Digital Library

Many Indiana school library media centers are developing web pages or portals to create a digital library that teachers and learners can access 24/7 (24 hours a day, seven days a week) in the LMC, in the classroom and from the home. These digital libraries provide not just access to the online catalog, but to full-text resources targeted at the school's curriculum and the needs of its users.

The following illustration briefly diagrams the components of a digital school library:

➢ The outer firewall provides a safe and nurturing environment.

➢ The core collection provides essential reference and periodical collections that are the "workhorses" of the digital information core (encyclopedias, Inspire, highly used Internet sites).

➢ The curriculum collection of digital resources matches the unique needs of the school and its learners and teachers.

➢ The elastic collection acts much like a phone card that opens expensive resources for a few hours of concentrated research and then closes the door when not in use.

➢ Access to the main Internet in various levels is approved and allowed by parents:
   o Level one - highly filtered access
   o Level two - More freedom
   o Level three - complete access

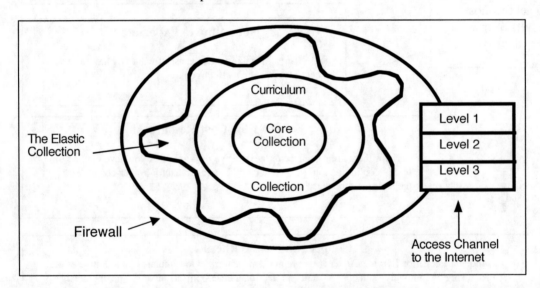

In addition to the information sources of the digital school library, the LMC portal should be the home page of every computer in the school. At this point, the LMC truly becomes the heart of the school as it is the "first and best place to look" before turning to Internet surfing. As a part of this library, collaborative units can be stored so that the portal becomes "the place for all my assignments (learner) or instructional units (teacher)." Further detail about the digital school library concept can be found at: http://www.indianalearns.org/

Will print libraries survive? Our users will tell us by their information behaviors.

Successful Strategies Using Information Technology to Enhance Learning

Many times, a simple set of flash cards is just as good as a $3,000 machine — and more reliable. Technological sophistication is not automatically the answer. Theoretically, technology should help students learn more and more efficiently, and should be a transparent part of the learning process.

Numerous publications tout effective ways to enhance learning through technology. In reality, they are idea starters. Each teaching team, library media specialist, technology specialist, and student group should, through trial and error, test a variety of techniques and showcase the best. Emphasize technology-based projects where substance is more important than flashy presentations; deep learning over surface learning. Consider the following strategies as a starter list:

Types of problems to create:

➢ **Collaborative Data Collection and Analysis** - Various student groups in the same school, in the community, state, nation, or internationally, collect data to solve an engaging problem.

➢ **Real Problems -** Numerous technologies allow students to handle "real" data to solve real problems. The data can be historical, contemporary, or obtained instantly through sensing devices.

➢ **Simulations** – Simulations, including simulation gaming, provide a way to come close to reality without encountering the dangers, the impossibilities of traveling in time or space, the "what ifs," or the risks.

Using Strategies:

➢ **The Novelty of Technology** - Enduring a steady diet of the same teaching strategies is boring. The use of a new technology or a fresh approach to an older technology can stimulate interest both in the technology itself and also in the subject matter to be mastered. Implementing new teaching strategies matched to appropriate technologies keeps the learning tasks fresh.

➢ **Communication Beyond the School** - The Internet, the amplified telephone, and e-mail allow students to communicate around the world, to other schools, experts, governments, agencies, libraries, museums, businesses and a host of other sources. This communication supports the learners as they explore ideas, concepts and important issues.

➢ **Multiple Data Sources** - The Internet, online databases, books, periodicals, video sources, and connections to other libraries help students experience a wide variety of information on the topic or question they are seeking. There is something for every student at every level.

To Stimulate:[1]

➢ **Inventive Thinking** – Use technology to stimulate curiosity, creativity and risk-taking and to promote higher-order thinking and sound reasoning.

➢ **Effective Communication** – Technology can stimulate teaming, collaboration, interactive communication, taking personal responsibility, and social responsibility.

➢ **High Productivity** – Encourage planning and managing for results as technological tools stimulate efficiency and as students learn to use real-world high-tech tools.

---

[1] Ideas for stimulation match many suggested in *NCREL's enGauge 21ˢᵗ Century Skills*. Naperville, IL: NCREL, 2002; also, November, Alan. *Empowering Students with Technology*. Arlington Heights, IL: Skylight, 2001.

Indiana Examples of
Enhancing Learning Through Technology

Here are three spotlights on excellent examples of learning experiences where technology has been an integral part.

From Persimmons to Pioneers
(Mitchell Community Schools, Muggs Murphy, project director)

Under a grant from the Indiana Dept. of Education, students and teachers from Mitchell Jr. and Sr. High Schools teamed with Spring Mill State Park officials and interested community members. These teams created materials that would promote the park and provide special activities for park visitors. They:
 ➢ Carved a wooden game for the visitor's center.
 ➢ Made a three-dimensional sign for the park (using CADD software).
 ➢ Created scrapbooks for the Nature Center.
 ➢ Produced HyperStudio stacks about the park for use by visitors (particularly those who are disabled and who cannot access certain parts of the park).
 ➢ Made videos about the park with music from the early time period of the area.

Teachers expected and got high motivation, real links to state standards, inter-disciplinary learning, creativity, community involvement, and a host of other benefits that a "real" project provides. Students have learned technology skills to build their research-based projects and the amount of research has been extensive. (email Muggs at: mugs@tima.com)

Courts in the Classroom
A product of the Indiana Judicial System and the Indiana Supreme Court, "Courts in the Classroom" provides curriculum concepts and other resources about Indiana's courts for the K-12 educator. Linked to Indiana curriculum standards, teachers and students can watch oral arguments, interact with featured cases, find a history of Indiana courts, ascertain the structure of Indiana courts, and access a video library. The site is particularly good to help students and adults put a human face on the courts and to interact through technology with real cases. At: http://www.in.gov/judiciary/education/

Project Hometown, Indiana
Hometown provides a chance for grades 3-5 to become "experts" on their community heritage and to publish their findings on the Internet. The project uses the historic Wabash-Erie Canal as a symbolic "information superhighway" to link students throughout the state. Students can do local history projects of many kinds to link to the web bank. Staff development is available for teachers who wish to enhance the Indiana history curriculum. At: http://wvec.k12.in.us/hometown

Leadership and Planning

The building-level technology leader sets the stage for the successful integration of technology into the school's instructional program. Leadership goes beyond the knowledge of computer hardware, software, networking, and staying on the cutting edge of systems.

Understanding the role.

Having a Sound Vision Linked to a Management Plan

Technology Standards for School Administrators published by ISTE describe six standards for solid technology leadership at the building and district levels
1. Leadership and Vision
2. Learning and Teaching
3. Productivity and Professional Practice
4. Support, Management, and Operations
5. Assessment and Evaluation
6. Social, Legal, and Ethical Issues

Source: Brooks-Young, Susan. *Making Technology Standards Work for You: A Guide for School Administrators.* Eugene, OR: ISTE, 2002.

What is our Local Progress with Leadership and Planning?

Lead by example.

Leading From a Position of Strength

Effective technology leaders at the building level model how technology can be used to enhance learning.

- ➢ They have a reputation of being able to come out from behind computer screens and networking devices to showcase real teaching and learning.
- ➢ They know how to integrate technology into collaboratively planned instructional units because they have a track record of doing so.
- ➢ They build a wide repertoire of successful learning experiences through technology to draw upon as they consult.

Lead through trust

Building a Track Record

Trust and confidence are earned over time with a faculty and learning community when:
- ➢ Technology systems are reliable and trustworthy over time.
- ➢ There is enough technical support to troubleshoot technical problems during the school day.
- ➢ Every teacher feels confident in using technology effectively.

Resource: *Making Technology Standards Work for You – A Guide for School Administrators.* Eugene, OR: ISTE, 2002. Contains valuable guidance not only for principals and superintendents, but technology specialists at both the school and district level.

Integrating Information Technology into the School as a Whole

When information technology is integrated into the total school community, what might an observer notice by touring the school, the library media center, or special areas of the school?

Student behaviors:

- ❑ Students are interested/engaged in learning projects using technological devices and print resources rather than using those devices for games/recreation.
- ❑ Students who are usually disinterested in school are engaged.
- ❑ Students are pursuing their own interests as a part of learning activities
- ❑ Because students are handling multiple data sources, they seem naturally headed in the direction of a problem-solving mode of learning.
- ❑ Students seem to be at ease using a variety of presentation technologies.
- ❑ Students are more focused on using the technology as a tool to further their learning than to "dress up" their projects or assignments.
- ❑ Other:

Facilities:

- ❑ Technology can be accessed from a variety of locations throughout the school. This arrangement allows for simultaneous use of technology by individual students, small groups, and large groups.
- ❑ Needed technologies are consistently available.
- ❑ Print resources and computer technologies are integrated into library media centers and classrooms.
- ❑ Technology is available to learners and teachers before and after school, and at noon, in addition to the regular school hours.
- ❑ Other:

Adults:

- ❑ Teachers, library media and technology specialists are committed to a technology-rich environment and feel comfortable teaching in that environment.
- ❑ Teachers, library media and technology specialists are coaching learners rather than delivering information.

For other items that could be added to the list above, consult *NCREL's enGauge: 21ˢᵗ Century Skills: Digital Literacies for a Digital Age*. Naperville, IL: NCREL, 2002.

The Eight-Step Vision for Professional Development in Technology

The booklet *Eight Steps to Highly Effective 'Next Generation' Professional Development for Learning Technology—Public Law 221 and Beyond* written in 2001by the IDOE is a practical guide for administrators to ensure that schools provide the professional development necessary to use technology effectively in the teaching and learning process as required by PL 221.

The Urgency for Digital Age Teaching and Learning From the *Eight Steps* Booklet:

Our children live in a digital world. They have never known a time without space travel, cell phones, MP3 quality sound, cloning, and, of course, instantaneous communication via email and the Internet. To them, technology is an accepted part of everyday life; the way television was to children of the 70s and 80's. Yet, while technology has had a tremendous impact on nearly every aspect of American society—especially the work place—the way teachers teach, students learn, and schools operate, remain virtually untouched by the digital age.

Educators of all kinds—school board members, parents, teachers, community leaders—are asking the question: "Are our graduates prepared to be successful in today's digital society?" While today, only a handful can answer, "Yes," in Indiana, the outlook is improving.

While Indiana does not require technology training for initial teacher licensure or teacher recertification, it is one of only eleven states that provides incentives for educators to use technology. In addition, the Buddy System Project gives computers to 4th graders who don't have them at home. This program also provides extensive professional development to teachers in the 60 participating schools. Because of programs like these, 87% of Indiana schools report that at least 50% of their teachers use a computer daily for planning and teaching. This compares favorably to a national average of 76%. Similarly, 53% of Indiana schools report that at least 50% of teachers use the Internet for instruction (Source: Market Data Retrieval, as reported in Technology Counts 2001).

At the U.S. Secretary of Education's 2000 conference, "Technology in Schools: Measuring the Impact and Shaping the Future," participants from across the country including classroom teachers, educational administrators, researchers, and policy leaders collectively reached the following conclusions:

> ➤ Breakthroughs in technology have advanced what we know about how children think and learn.
> ➤ Research shows that, under the right conditions, technology can increase children's academic achievement.
> ➤ Technology's tremendous influence on society has changed what children need to know and be able to do to be successful.
> ➤ Educators should use technology to more accurately assess what children are learning successfully, what they are not learning successfully, and why.

The challenge is to translate these realities into the daily learning experiences of children in every classroom in Indiana. Succeeding will require the 'next generation' professional development—new pathways to thoughtful, meaningful teaching, learning, and leading in a digital age.

The Eight Steps

1. Create a shared vision for digital age learning.

2. Set professional development goals that build toward the vision.

3. Assess the readiness of teachers based on agreed upon metrics.

4. Link 'next generation' strategies to professional development goals.

5. Identify time and resources available for professional development.

6. Think systems— Build a professional development master plan.

7. Establish conditions essential for teachers to implement what they learn.

8. Systematically assess and report progress.

Professional Development for Technology

Here are listed a sample of valuable professional development opportunities for Indiana library media specialists and technology specialists. Other professional development resources will be found at this book's website at www.indianalearns.org.

- ❑ **Office of Learning Resources** (OLR), Indiana Department of Education, provides professional development opportunities throughout the year. Regional Contact Meetings, for both library media and technology specialists, are held in the fall, winter, and spring - in eight sections of the state. These meetings provide opportunities for media and technology coordinators to share ideas and learn from colleagues. Each spring free regional workshops for classroom teachers, library media and technology specialists are presented across the state. At: http://www.doe.state.in.us/olr/techmeetings/welcome.html.

- ❑ **Association for Media Educators** (AIME) – Annual conference in the fall; pre-conferences and concurrent sessions on a variety of instruction media and technology topics including integration of technology with academic standards At: http://www.ilfonline.org/Conf/AIME%20Conf/index.htm

- ❑ **Education Service Centers** offer professional development opportunities around the state. Check the web site of the Service Center in your region for specific activities. At: http://doe.state.in.us/esc/welcome

- ❑ **The Buddy2 Teaching and Learning Center** provides professional development opportunities for Indiana educators to share best teaching and learning practices that combine technology with curriculum to increase student academic achievement. There is currently no or a small charge for participation. Topics include: Making Friends with Data, Technology Integration: What to Do, Writing with Technology Tools. At: **http://www.btlc.org**

- ❑ **Indiana Web Academy's** mission is to empower the students, parents, and educators in the State of Indiana to integrate technology and the Internet with education. Offers one-hour seminars on Microsoft Word, Internet Fundamentals, creating and maintaining web pages and weeklong summer courses for graduate credit. At: http://indianawebacademy.org/training.asp

- ❑ **WebQuest for Staff Developers** involves participants in a team planning activity. At: http://faculty.nl.edu/mhan/NECC99Web/sdwebquest.htm

- ❑ **IHETS**, the Indiana Higher Education Telecommunication System, created by the General Assembly to permit sharing of educational resources via technology, posts Web Based Education Guides at www.ihets.org/consortium/k12/guides.htmln Guides provide guidelines and tools for creating web pages, WebQuests, and acceptable use policies.

- ❑ *Eight Steps to Highly Effective 'Next Generation' Professional Development for Learning and Technology* WebQuest available at http://ideanet.doe.state.in.us/olr/eightsteps/welcome.html help educators design professional development programs to meet the requirements of P.L. 221.

- ❑ **ICONnect** provides a variety of free online courses that offer skills to navigate the Web and use search engines effectively. The courses explore issues raised by Internet use in the classroom and provide ideas for integrating Internet resources into the curriculum. Designed specifically for school library media specialists, teachers and students, the courses can be used as building blocks for developing school based Internet workshops. At: http://www.ala.org/ICONN/onlineco.html

- ❑ **NCRTEC** gathers professional development materials including *Blueprints,* a practical toolkit to help schools, districts, and other providers design and facilitate effective professional development. They also provide *Captured Wisdom*™: examples of real educators and learners using successful practices of technology. At: www.ncrtec.org/ pd/index.html

Assessment of Technology's Impact

Both learners and teachers are often quite willing to invest time and effort to integrate technology when it is accessible and it works. Collecting, reviewing, and reporting data at the organizational level, the teaching unit level and the learner level will help assess the impact technology is ready to make and is making in the school.

Level of Measure	Factor	Sources of Data
Technology at the Organization Level (District vision for effective technology use)	The state of the technology infrastructure in the district and at the building/ LMC/ classrooms	❑ Percent of learners who could find an Internet ready computer when needed. ❑ Number and percent of operational computer connections in the LMC. ❑ The annual budget to upgrade networks to meet technology plan needs. ❑ The size and competence of the technology staff for the school. ❑ Percent of staff who know the technology vision.
Technology at the Learning Unit Level (class interaction and use)	Technology's contribution to the teaching and learning.	❑ The percent of students who would rate the technology as helpful in completing their assignments during a unit of instruction. ❑ The number and percent of teachers who would report during a sample month that technology had "contributed to learning" during a collaborative activity in the LMC.
Technology at the Learner Level (as individuals)	Individual progress by each learner as technology becomes a trusted tool.	❑ Rubric score for use of technology in a project. ❑ Rubric score that content knowledge was enhanced through technology. ❑ Rubric score that information literacy standards were met.

Helpful publications for more measures to consider:

➢ *NCREL's enGauge: 21st Century Skills: Digital Literacies for a Digital Age.* Naperville, IL: NCREL, 2002.

➢ Jones, Beau Fly, et. al. *Plugging In: Choosing and Using Educational Technology.* Oakbrook, IL: NCREL, 1995.

➢ "Technology in Schools: Guidelines for Assessing Technology in Education." A publication of the National Center for Education Statistics, U.S. Dept. of Education, November, 2002. At: http://nces.ed.gov/

➢ Johnston, Jerome and Linda Toms Barker, eds. *Assessing the Impact of Technology in Teaching and Learning: A Sourcebook for Evaluators.* Ann Arbor, MI: University of Michigan, Institute for Social Research, 2002.

➢ *Planning for DET (Data-Driven Decisions About Technology).* Naperville, IL: NCREL, 1999.

➢ *Technology Counts* - A yearly report focusing on how technology is changing education. At: http://www.edweek.org/sreports/tc02/

➢ For more resources on assessment, see the web page for this book at http://www.indianalearns.org and http://ideanet.doe.state.in.us/technology

Reflecting With Students:
A Learning Unit Level Assessment

Why Reflect?
Frank discussions and reflections with learners can provide a great deal of valuable feedback from learners as they try to use technology to accomplish their assignments. Being a coach rather than a dictator can be quite beneficial as systems are created, maintained, and modified.

Who would conduct the reflection?
A mix of the teachers, administrators, the library media specialist, the technology specialist, plus the learners themselves.

When should the reflection happen?
➢ After a learning activity where technology, information systems, LMC facilities and resources were a critical part of the learning experience.
➢ After the grades are in. (Students should feel free to speak up.)
➢ After an assessment where learners had to demonstrate their knowledge or what they did.

What questions might be constructed to ask during a reflection?
Each reflection will have its own set of questions, but the list below is suggestive of topics to broach and adapt to any grade level:
➢ Here is the state standard/local expectation that we as teachers had for this learning experience (list those used by all teachers and specialists across the various curricular standards). How well do you feel we did as a group in meeting those objectives?
➢ How well did a certain technology help you as a learner?
➢ What information sources or systems seemed to help you the most?
➢ What problems did you encounter with either a technology or information sources?
➢ What could we do to make sure that technology and information sources serve us better in our future projects?
➢ How could you help the process more as learners?

How sophisticated should the reflection be?
Tailor the reflection to the maturation level and student experience using technology.

How much time should it take?
Reflections might be as short as ten minutes or as long as a half hour depending on the complexity of the learning activity, the difficulties encountered, and the sophistication level of the learners.

➢ **What should happen after the reflection?**
➢ Meet with the other adults involved to plan any changes in program.
➢ Document the reflection as a part of data-driven practice at the learning unit level.

Bottom Line Questions

➢ What is the sophistication level of the students in their use of technology?

➢ Is the use of technology really enhancing the learning experience?

Judging Glitz vs. Content in Hi-Tech Products at the Learner Level

It is easy to be impressed with the glitz of technology particularly when the student knows more about computers or other high-tech than we do. But glitz is not a substitute for deep learning. Thus the first two commandments of the ten commandments for judging projects for the media fair and for classroom products:[1]

> 1. Thou shalt notice the substance of the product or project first.
> 2. Thou shalt notice technological expertise later.

As learners begin projects, the collaborating team constructs a rubric that sets content before format; rewards learning over presentation; process over product.

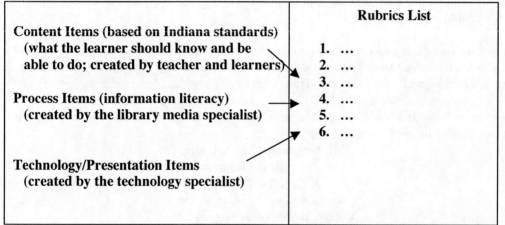

Content Items (based on Indiana standards)
(what the learner should know and be able to do; created by teacher and learners)

Process Items (information literacy)
(created by the library media specialist)

Technology/Presentation Items
(created by the technology specialist)

Rubrics List

1. …
2. …
3. …
4. …
5. …
6. …

Rubric generators are available from NCRtec to assist collaboration teams in including desirable elements. For example, a holistic scoring guide for a compare/contrast project resulted in numerous items of which one is listed below. See at: http://www.ncrtec.org/t1/sgsp.index.html

	5 Exemplary	4 Not Quite Exemplary	3 Developed	2 Not Quite Developed	1 Limited
Content Knowledge	The purpose/main point is clearly defined. The student demonstrates strong critical thinking and well integrated ideas, and maintains clear focus and a compelling and original voice. The student compares and contrasts two things using specific examples to support his position. There is evidence of genuine learning - others find work useful and benefit from this product.		The main point is only implied or partially stated. The student shows some evidence of critical thinking and integration, as well as focus, style, and voice. The student compares and contrasts two things but uses few or somewhat unclear examples to support his position. There is new learning but for the student only – not developed or useful for others.		The main point is unclear. There is little or no evidence of critical thinking or integration and a lack of focus, style, and voice. The student does not compare / contrast two things, and uses inappropriate or no examples to support his position. There is no evidence of new learning - nor developed or useful for student or others.

Resource: Simkins, Michael, et.al. *Increasing Student Learning Through Multimedia Projects*. Alexandria, VA: ASCD, 2002. See also NWREL products at http://www.nwrel.org/assessment/

---

[1] What are the other eight commandments, you follow?

CREATING AN INFORMATION LITERATE LEARNER

Definition: Information literacy has been defined in a variety of ways, and while some details vary, the central substance has not.

Information Power, the major standards document of the school library field, defines information literacy as the effective users of ideas and information.[1] Doyle's popular definition is "the ability to access, evaluate, and use information from a variety of sources."[2] A recent review of the research on information literacy by Loertscher and Woolls looks at many models and their application with children and teenagers.[3] For this publication, the information literate student possesses five qualities of mind and skill:

An Organized Investigator

A Critical Thinker

A Creative Thinker

An Effective Communicator

A Responsible Information User

One of the major agendas of the school library media profession is to assist students as they are introduced to an information rich environment and provide them with the research skills they need to survive. Library media and technology specialists are interested in a certain quality of mind, a broadened capacity of information handling, an internalized model of personal research, and an ability to be a good citizen in the information world.

Library media and technology specialists also know that the best way to teach the research process is to collaborate with teachers and teach the process "just in time" when learners must do projects assigned in the classroom.

Because information literacy is a newer, but key concept in education, the balance of this section covers this concept in more depth.

---

[1] American Association of School Librarians and Association for Educational Communications and Technology. *Information Power: Building Partnerships for Learning*. Chicago: American Library Association, 1998.

[2] Doyle, Christina S. *Information Literacy in an Information Society: A Concept for the Information Age*. ERIC Clearinghouse on Information and Technology, June 1994.

[3] Loertscher, David V. and Blanche Woolls. *Information Literacy: A Review of the Research*. 2nd ed. Hi Willow Research and Publishing, 2002.

An Organized Investigator

Traditionally, students have done little "research" or investigation until high school. However, the advent of rich information environments allows all students the opportunity to develop investigative strategies and become problem solvers and meet state standards at the same time.

Beginning inquirers need some guidance in developing a process for doing research. Each student can be introduced to a research process model adopted by the faculty for the school. Popular models include the Eisenberg & Berkowitz Big Six Skills, the I-Search Process created by K. Macronie, *Information Power* (1998 ed*),* and the California School Library Association Information Literacy Model.[1]   Loertscher's and the AASL information literacy model are presented below.

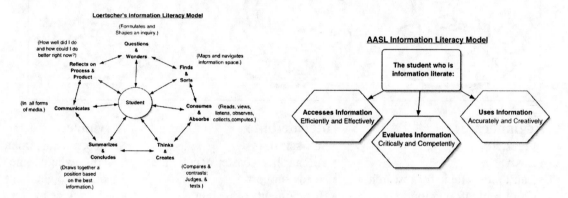

After several research experiences using a research model, learners can then develop their own model to match their individual learning style. The library media specialist should have numerous examples of research process models available for consideration by the faculty and can take the lead in teaching this concept to the faculty as a whole. An effective activity with faculty is to present them with numerous information literacy models and then challenge them to develop their own in an hour-long professional development session. This gives them not only a sense of their own investigative style, but also a much clearer notion of what information literacy is and how it can be used in their own research.

Resources:
➢ *Inspire: What Do You Want to Know Today? Teacher Resource Guide.* At: http://www.inspire.net This guide contains a number of information literacy models created in Indiana and sample lessons for teaching information literacy in various curricular areas using the Inspire databases.
➢ Koechlin, Carol and Sandi Zwaan. *InfoTasks for Successful Learning.* Portland, ME: Stenhouse, 2001. Contains a variety of information literacy lessons arranged in topical order by the type of information task learners are confronting. Also available from LMC Source at www.lmcsource.com

---

[1] One of the best sources for information literacy guidance is: *From Library Skills to Information Literacy,* 2nd ed. (1997), authored by the California School Library Association and available from LMC Source, P.O. Box 131266, Spring TX 77393. Another valuable publication from the same company containing many information literacy models is *Information Literacy: A Review of the Research* 2nd ed. by David Loertscher and Blanche Woolls. Hi Willow, 2002.

How to Help Learners Become Organized Investigators

Children and young adults at any age can begin learning the techniques of conducting inquiries and solving the problems they meet. Using scope and sequence charts of what learners are to know or do at a given grade level, professionals can assess learner sophistication levels easily. Students may be beginners, intermediates or advanced information literates no matter the age, gender, cultural background, or principal language spoken. It is not difficult to recognize the difference in sophistication.

Beginners
- Frazzled
- Lost
- Can't pick a topic for research
- Can't find information
- Desperately needs help
- Needs help constantly
- Distracted
- Uninterested

Intermediate
- Self-starting
- Still a roller-coaster experience
- Needs support
- Has moments of insight
- Interested
- Somewhat systematic
- Will take advice

Advanced
- Independent learner
- Knows where to go and how to get there
- Asks advice to monitor progress

Instead of regimenting the teaching of investigative strategies, the classroom teacher and the library media specialist might try the following with a whole group, small groups, or individual learners:

➤ Teach a research model as a whole several times at varying intervals. Students will proceed through a problem in a step-by-step fashion and discuss each step as the investigation proceeds and is completed.

➤ After a research project or inquiry, reflect on the model students have used. At an appropriate time, have students create their own information literacy model. Models will vary since learning styles vary.

➤ Teach students that real research is generally a very messy process—there are many false starts, problems encountered, progress, backtracking, and enough hassles to require a great deal of patience and hard work.

➤ Have students test their own model on a second project. Refine.

➤ When students complete a project, assign a grade for both the process and the product. Students should know in advance, via a rubric, that both the process and the product will be assessed.

A Critical Thinker

Library media specialists see critical thinking as one of the major components of the information literate person. The ISTEP+ and other national tests such as the ACT and SAT have many items that test not only factual knowledge, but also the ability to think critically about a concept. Instead of advocating an add-on to the curriculum—a new scope and sequence or curriculum to be taught— critical thinking is best integrated into the subjects and projects at hand.

Teachers and library media specialists should teach critical thinking strategies within the context of content-area projects, lessons, and information use. The objective is to create neither students who are sponges (believing everything they read, view, and hear), nor cynics (believing nothing they read, view, and hear), but healthy skeptics (using evidence and authoritative sources to judge believability).

CRITICAL THINKING CONTINUUM

Sponges - - - - - - - - - - **Healthy Skeptics** - - - - - - - - - - **Cynics**

A Major Challenge: Evaluating Information on the Internet

One of the major challenges, for example, is to educate learners to evaluate information they find on the Internet. Teachers and library media specialists should work together to teach learners these evaluative skills developmentally. Very young users may simply be asked to decide whether a site seems to be on the right topic or whether it is easy to understand. As learners develop cognitively and become more sophisticated in their use of online resources, teachers and library media specialists should respond with increasingly sophisticated lessons about authority, bias, currency and accuracy.

As Students Become More Sophisticated, So Do the Questions We Ask of Them

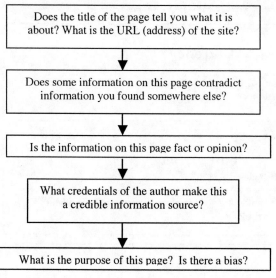

Does the title of the page tell you what it is about? What is the URL (address) of the site?

↓

Does some information on this page contradict information you found somewhere else?

↓

Is the information on this page fact or opinion?

↓

What credentials of the author make this a credible information source?

↓

What is the purpose of this page? Is there a bias?

Resources for Web Evaluation

1. "Critical Evaluation Information," by Kathy Schrock. At: http://school.discovery.com/ schrockguide/eval.html
2. Cyber Guides, by Linda Joseph. At: http://www.cyberbee.com/guides.html
3. Infopeople's "Evaluating Internet Resources." At: http://infopeople.berkeley.edu/how to/bkmk/select.html
4. "Teaching Critical Evaluation Skills for World Wide Web Resources," by Jane Alexander and Marsha Tate. At: http://www2.widener.edu/ Wolfgram-Memorial-Library/ webevaluation/ webeval.htm

Website Evaluation Guide for Learners

Building a useful guide, handout, tip sheet, wallet card, or online evaluation form for students can help them evaluate the information they get from the Internet. Indiana University has created guidelines for undergraduate students that might be helpful in the creation of a local guide. At: http://www.indiana.edu/~libugls/Publications/webeval.html

---

What is the purpose of the Web site?

Do a quick scan of the site. Can you determine its general purpose? Is it meant to:

> **INFORM**   e.g., about current events, new information, etc.
> **EXPLAIN**   e.g., teach, instruct, etc.
> **PERSUADE**   e.g., change your mind, sell you something, etc.

Resource:

Valenza's Guidelines For Teaching Web Evaluation:

1. Students must evaluate their search tools.
2. Students must evaluate their result lists.
3. Students must evaluate an author's credentials.
4. Students must holistically evaluate the sites they plan to use.

From:
Valenza, Joyce Kasman. "Evaluating Web Resources," *Classroom Connect*, February 2002, p. 4-7.

Website Evaluation Questions

Accuracy
- Is the information accurate?
- Has the information been edited/fact-checked?
- Is the information verifiable?
- Does the site document the sources used?
- If the information is historical or geographical, are the dates of events accurate?
- How does the information compare with what you already know?

Authority
- Does the site have an author?
- What are the author's qualifications or expertise in the area?
- Is the contact information for the author or the sponsor/publisher given?
- What is the relationship between the author and the sponsoring institution?

Currency
- Is the site up-to-date?
- When was the information created or last updated?
- Are the links expired or current?

Point of View
- Whose point of view/perspective is given?
- Is the author simply promoting an agenda?
- To what extent is the information trying to sway the opinion of the audience?
Is there advertising on the page?

WebQuests and Web Explorations: Two Strategies for Research

Learners often face a set of common problems as they face a research assignment. Three common ones are:

➢ No solid sense of the research process.
➢ Too much time spent finding information, not enough time analyzing, evaluating, and synthesizing it.
➢ Indiscriminate use of information sources without evaluating them.

Two strategies to provide the learner with supportive scaffolding:

WebQuests

WebQuests are web-based assignments that engage students in interesting and preferably real-world problem solving linked to state standards.

Elements of a WebQuest:

An introduction that sets the stage and provides some background information.
A task that is achievable and engaging.
A set of information resources (online, print, etc.) selected by the teacher and library media specialist needed to complete the task.
A description of the process the learners should go through in accomplishing the task.
Some guidance on how to organize the information acquired.
An evaluation, often a rubric, designed to measure results.
A conclusion that brings closure to the quest, reminds students of what they've learned, and encourages them to extend the experience.

WebQuests Work Well When They:

Promote critical thinking with emphasis on essential questions.
Stimulates effective cooperative learning
Structure complicated research assignments
Take advantage of online resources without leading students on a wild goose chase.

Source: Douglas Achterman's revision of Bernie Dodge's "Some Thought's About WebQuests," At: http://edweb.sdsu.edu/courses/edtec596/about_webquests.html.

Web Explorations

Web explorations begin with a state standard and then provide activities that require an information-rich environment.

Elements of a Web Exploration:

An introduction that sets forth the learning expectation based on state standards.
A task that is achievable and engaging.
A rubric to assess success.
A set of information resources (online, print, etc.) pre-selected by the teacher and library media specialist.
Encouragement and instruction on finding and evaluating additional resources online.
Clear instructions concerning an individual or group product.
A culminating experience designed to capitalize on what everyone learned.
A reflection about the contribution of web and other online resources.

Web Explorations Work Well When They:

Allows for a wider variety of activities and strategies than do WebQuests.
Promote both pre-selected and self-selected information resource utilization.
Can begin on the Web, but can be designed to go far beyond that resource.

Resource: Bernie Dodge's WebQuest site at: http://webquest.sdsu.edu/webquest.html

A WebQuest Example: Lee Ann Richardson designed a WebQuest for 4th Graders entitled "Will It Rain on My Party?" where students try to plan a surprise birthday party but must predict the weather before deciding on location and activities. At: http://www.ips.k12.in.us/webquest/3/ss/spring01/richardson/webquest.html.

A Creative Thinker

Learning is often so regimented with students receiving points for molding projects to exact specifications that creativity is penalized. Recognizing and rewarding creative thinking even when the student might act like Jim Carey or Robin Williams is a major challenge. Is it being encouraged in collaborative units in the library media center? Consider the definition of creativity at the right[1] and a statement concerning inventive thinking from enGauge:[2]

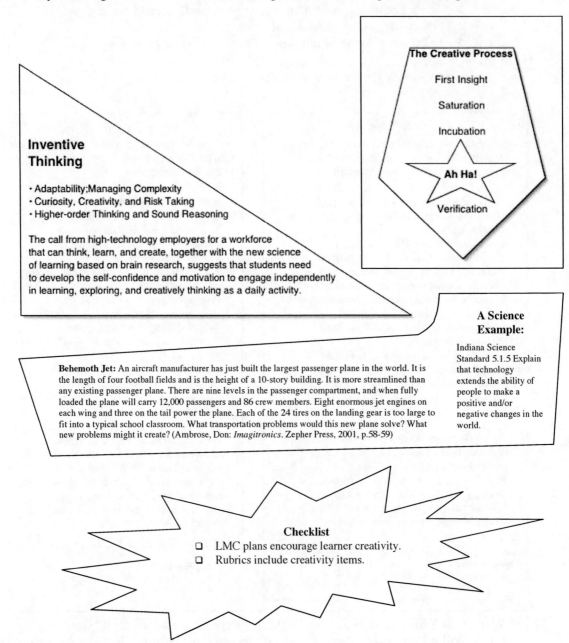

The Creative Process

First Insight

Saturation

Incubation

Ah Ha!

Verification

Inventive Thinking

• Adaptability;Managing Complexity
• Curiosity, Creativity, and Risk Taking
• Higher-order Thinking and Sound Reasoning

The call from high-technology employers for a workforce that can think, learn, and create, together with the new science of learning based on brain research, suggests that students need to develop the self-confidence and motivation to engage independently in learning, exploring, and creatively thinking as a daily activity.

A Science Example:

Indiana Science Standard 5.1.5 Explain that technology extends the ability of people to make a positive and/or negative changes in the world.

Behemoth Jet: An aircraft manufacturer has just built the largest passenger plane in the world. It is the length of four football fields and is the height of a 10-story building. It is more streamlined than any existing passenger plane. There are nine levels in the passenger compartment, and when fully loaded the plane will carry 12,000 passengers and 86 crew members. Eight enormous jet engines on each wing and three on the tail power the plane. Each of the 24 tires on the landing gear is too large to fit into a typical school classroom. What transportation problems would this new plane solve? What new problems might it create? (Ambrose, Don: *Imagitronics*. Zepher Press, 2001, p.58-59)

Checklist

❑ LMC plans encourage learner creativity.
❑ Rubrics include creativity items.

---

[1] The creative process is Getzel/Kneller's description in von Wodtke, Mark. *Mind Over Media: Creative Thinking Skills for Electronic Media*. New York: McGraw-Hill, 1993, p. 115.

[2] *NCREL's enGauge: 21st Century Skills: Digital Literacies for a Digital Age*. Naperville, IL: NCREL, 2002, p. 23.

An Effective Communicator

Learners should be able to express themselves and communicate their findings successfully in a wide variety of media including:

> Written reports
> Term papers
> Web sites
> Multimedia presentations
> Video presentations
> Graphic charts, diagrams, transparencies, PowerPoint presentations, etc.
> Real and constructed objects
> Reenactments, drama, oral presentations
> Portfolios

Effective Communication

Interactive communication is the ability to convey, exchange, transmit, access, and understand information. In today's wired, networked society it is imperative that students understand how to communicate using technology.

Source: *NCREL's enGauge*. Naperville IL: NCREL, 2001, p. 33

Learner products not only should span the various types of media but also should become increasingly sophisticated as experience with technology increases. As a normal part of product creation, learners expect to be assessed on their communication expertise. Here are sample high-point statements on a rubric:

My product:
> Reports clearly the question or quest.
> Reports the various information sources I used.
> Draws from excellent information sources.
> Reflects my thinking about the topic covered.
> Is a summary of what I have learned.
> Uses technology well.
> Is neat and organized.
> Is presented well.

Checklist
- Technology and library media specialists recommend rubric statements concerning product quality to teachers during the planning of collaborative unit experiences.
- Rubric statements (and thus student expectations) cover both the technical quality of the product as well as how well content learning is communicated.
- Product sophistication across the various technology increases across the grade levels.
- Learners are expected to be able to use a widening array of communication technologies as they progress through school.
- The school provides a wide range of reliable communication technologies, both low- and high-tech to its learners.
- Just-in-time instruction is given to learners in using communication technologies for assignments.

A Responsible Information User

When only a textbook, some note paper, and a few library reference books were available as the chief student information sources, the need to teach responsible information use was not a common part of education. Now, however, as the information pool deepens, students of all ages handle vast quantities of information resources. They are citizens of multiple networks and with that citizenship comes more responsibility. Each member of the professional team must coach students in the behaviors that respect intellectual property, understand "fair use," and also build the creativity needed to publish one's own work.

Roles of the Professional Staff and Learners

Information Coaches Behavior
(teachers, library media specialists, technology specialists):
- ❑ Model concepts.
- ❑ Teach concepts both jointly and individually.
- ❑ Reinforce each other's teaching.
- ❑ Assess student progress in responsibility.

Learner Responsibility
- ➢ Creating assignments where cut and clip doesn't work.
- ➢ Teaching the concept of intellectual property and copyright.
- ➢ Teaching paraphrasing, quoting, citations.
- ➢ Teaching style manuals.
- ➢ Teaching both plagiarism and fair use.
- ➢ Building creative expression, voice, and publishing one's work in print and online.
- ➢ Respecting equipment, networks, and online citizenship through acceptable use policies.
- ➢ Becoming more sophisticated over time in products, communication ability, and the creation of intellectual property and the use of other's property.

Resource:
- ➢ "How to Cite" (Inspire) provides learners with numerous helps in citing all types of media and in a variety of editorial styles. At: www.inspire.net/cite.html

Collaborative Teaching of Information Literacy: Possible Scenarios

Teaching information literacy is a joint responsibility of teacher and library media specialist and is never done except as it applies to an information skill to meet a state standard. Here are a few possible scenarios.

As soon as learners become comfortable with an information literacy model, they are encouraged by both teacher and library media specialist to modify the model to suit their own learning style.

Teachers and library media specialists agree on an information literacy model to be taught throughout the school.

During the first research project of the year, the library media specialist teaches the model (or reviews it) while teacher listens and learns the model.

Learners may first apply the info. Lit. model in language. arts, then apply it in a social studies project and later a science project.

Teachers and library media specialists assess whether learners are becoming more sophisticated over time and plan accordingly.

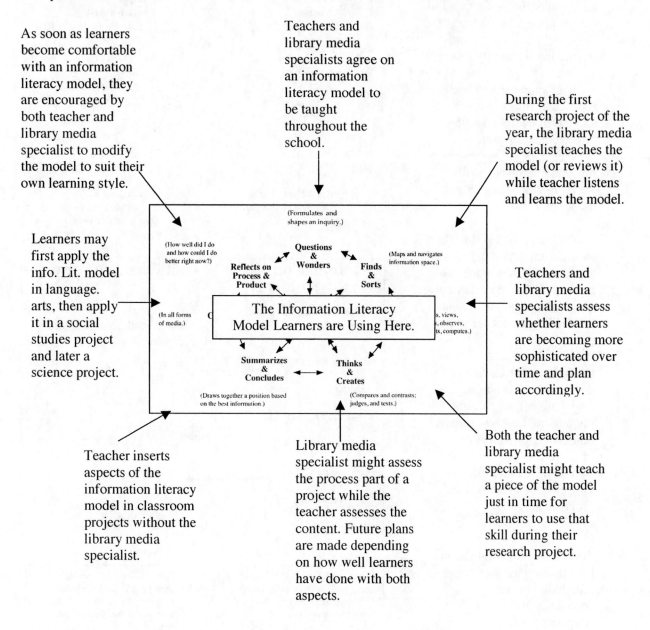

(Formulates and shapes an inquiry.)

(How well did I do and how could I do better right now?)

Questions & Wonders

(Maps and navigates information space.)

Reflects on Process & Product

Finds & Sorts

(In all forms of media.)

The Information Literacy Model Learners are Using Here.

s, views, , observes, ts, computes.)

Summarizes & Concludes

Thinks & Creates

(Draws together a position based on the best information.)

(Compares and contrasts; judges, and tests.)

Teacher inserts aspects of the information literacy model in classroom projects without the library media specialist.

Library media specialist might assess the process part of a project while the teacher assesses the content. Future plans are made depending on how well learners have done with both aspects.

Both the teacher and library media specialist might teach a piece of the model just in time for learners to use that skill during their research project.

Methods of Teaching Information Literacy

Library media specialists teaching information literacy have sometimes succumbed to the temptation of teaching those skills as a course of instruction or "library lesson."

Such an approach has been rejected as time consuming and inefficient. Rather, the professional literature recommends the integration of information literacy skills at the point when learners will use them.

As the illustration at the right shows, sometimes this teaching will take place as a mini-lesson when students are assigned a project and come to the library media center to do research.

However, if the teacher is doing an inquiry unit or a major project, the information literacy teaching will form the scaffolding of the entire research process. There will be a number of information mini-lessons as the research progresses.

In either method, the illustration at the right shows how the two agendas are co-mingled to insure accountability for both educators.

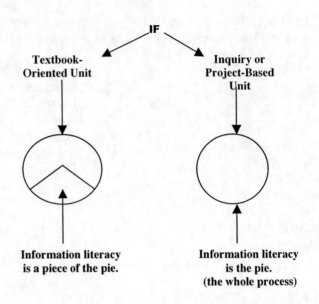

IF

Textbook-Oriented Unit

Inquiry or Project-Based Unit

Information literacy is a piece of the pie.

Information literacy is the pie. (the whole process)

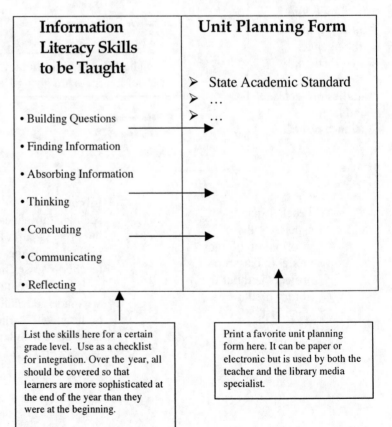

Information Literacy Skills to be Taught

Unit Planning Form

➢ State Academic Standard
➢ …
➢ …

• Building Questions

• Finding Information

• Absorbing Information

• Thinking

• Concluding

• Communicating

• Reflecting

List the skills here for a certain grade level. Use as a checklist for integration. Over the year, all should be covered so that learners are more sophisticated at the end of the year than they were at the beginning.

Print a favorite unit planning form here. It can be paper or electronic but is used by both the teacher and the library media specialist.

Indiana Information Literacy Correlations

Technology skills have been embedded into the Indiana state standards documents. Information literacy skills in the standards may not be immediately apparent. Thus, teams of library media specialists have been creating correlation documents that identify opportunities within the various state standards appropriate places to integrate the various information literacy skills and which skills seem the most appropriate.[1]

Since information literacy is "learning how to learn," most opportunities to integrate into a state standard goal are present in the "verbs" of the standards statement. For example:

> <u>Distinguish</u> between realistic and non-objective works of art and <u>recognize</u> the <u>identifying</u> [identify] characteristics of both. (Visual Arts K.6.1)

Thus, an easy way to discover a role for the library media specialist or the technology specialist is to do two things:

Recognize the verbs in standards statements as clues. Recognize the difference between content knowledge and process knowledge – the latter being part of the domain of information literacy.

Many library media specialists and technology specialists concentrate on "working on the teacher's agenda" or teaching the state standards rather than considering information literacy or technology skills as a separate curriculum with their own demands on time in the school schedule. Thus, during collaborative planning, all the teaching partners recognize content and process parts of the state standard and plans to teach both during the unit are made.

Resource:

> ➤ Koechlin, Carol and Sandi Zwaan. *InfoTasks for Successful Learning: Building Skills in Reading, Writing, and Research*. Portland, ME: Stenhouse, 2001. Arranged in dictionary order by skill topic, each page presents examples of teaching and integrating a particular skill into various units of instruction across the disciplines.

Bottom Line:

Everyone in the school is aware that information literacy and technology skills are natural parts of the learning process.

---

[1] Correlations have been done for Visual Arts, Music, Social Studies, and Physical Education (published and available from the Indiana Department of Education and online at: http://doe.state.in.us/standards/ILS_Correlations.html)

INFO-LIT TASK VERBS

Accesses
Analyze
Apply
Appreciate
Ask
Compare
Connect
Construct
Contrast
Create
Critique
Demonstrate
Describe
Discriminate
Discuss
Distinguish
Evaluate
Examine
Expand
Experience
Find
Formulate
Generate
Identify
Integrate
Judge
Know
Listen
Locate
Make
Match
Participates
Practice
Present
Process
Pursue
Read
Recognize
Refine
Reflect
Reflects
Research
Respond
Search
Speculate
Think
Understand
Use
Utilize
Visit
Write

Professional Development for Information Literacy

➤ **Ball State** offers courses on campus as well as via distance learning including; "Information Resources in Libraries" and "Methods and Materials for School Library Media Centers." At: www.bsu.edu

➤ **Better Information Literacy**, a section of the Maryland Department of Education's Project BETTER series, which pulls together research about information literacy instruction to show how it supports effective learning. At: www.mdk12.org/practices/good_instruction/projectbetter/information_literacy

➤ **Big6**, an approach to teaching information skills, web site provides a description of this model, lessons, resources and a chart correlating the Big6 skills with the national Information Literacy Standards developed by the American Association of School Librarians and the National Educational Standards for Students (NETS). At: www.big6.com

➤ **Buddy2 Teaching and Learning Center** in Indianapolis offers two all day workshops for IN educators on information literacy: "Learning to Learn: Making Effective Use of Student Research" and 'Information Literacy Skills for Today's Students". There is no charge for these courses. At: www.btlc.org

➤ **CyberTours,** created by Pam Berger InfoSearch editor, is a series of activities designed to provide a hands-on exploration of search strategies, information sources and issues. At: www.infosearcher.com/ cybertours

➤ **From Now On**, a free educational technology journal, published by Jamie McKenzie, provides on going information about information literacy. An example is "Winning with Information Literacy" (Summer 2000) describes how moving past technology to literacy will improve student achievement. At: www.fno.org

➤ **Indiana State University** delivers many courses via distance learning. Titles include "Reference Sources and Services for Library Media" and 'Instructional Media for Elementary Teaching." At: http://soe.indstate.edu/cimt/

➤ **Indiana University School of Library and Information Science** at Bloomington and Indianapolis offers graduate courses and special workshops on information literacy topics including; "Information Inquiry for School Teachers", "Information Sources and Services," and Education of information Users." At: www.slis.Indiana.edu/

➤ **TILT,** Texas Information literacy Tutorial, is an educational web site designed to introduce users research sources and skills. A good beginning to understand information literacy, selecting sources, searching skills, and criteria for assessing credibility of sources. At: http://titl.lib.utsystem.edu

➤ **"21st Century Literacies"** Pacific Bell/UCLA Initiatives for 21st Century Literacy, 2002. - Contains resources both bibliographic and web-based to assist library media specialists in their quest to learn and/or teach literacy skills. Contains many lessons for information literacy, media literacy, multicultural literacy, and visual literacy. At http://www.kn.pacbell.com/wired/2stcent/

Assessment of Information Literacy

Both learners and teachers are often quite willing to invest time and effort to integrate information literacy into lessons, believing that "content learning" is paramount. However, analysis of state standards and standardized tests reveals that information literacy is indeed a part of the total expectation for learners. Collecting, reviewing, and reporting data at the organizational level, the teaching unit level and the learner level will help assess the impact information literacy is ready to make and is making in the school.

Level of Measure	Factor	Sources of Data
Information literacy at the Organization Level (District and School)	The state of information literacy in the school and district.	❑ Evidence that district and school library media professionals have plans in place to deliver information literacy as a part of the state standards. ❑ Evidence that professional development opportunities exist to assist teachers and library media specialists to integrate information literacy into the curriculum. ❑ Evidence that scheduling, planning time, and other organizational factors allow information literacy to be a regular part of instruction. ❑ Evidence that state information literacy correlation documents have been considered in local information literacy plans.
Information literacy at the Learning Unit Level (class interaction and use)	The success that the class and the teacher experience during a unit of instruction both in the classroom and the LMC when information literacy is integrated into the learning experience.	❑ The percent of students who followed an information literacy model as a guide during a research project. ❑ The percent of learners who logged their way through a research project and drew their own information literacy model. (see p. 108) ❑ The percent of the faculty that could be categorized as successful integrators of information literacy into learning. ❑ The number and percent of time during a sample month that information literacy could be said to have "contributed to learning" during collaborative activities in the LMC
Information literacy at the Learner Level (as individuals)	Individual progress by each learner as information literacy becomes a trusted strategy in each learner's education.	❑ Rubric score that an individual used information literacy to enhance a project after being taught its use. ❑ Rubric score that content knowledge was enhanced through information literacy. ❑ Rubric score that the local standards for technology literacy and information literacy were met.

Logging and Assessing the Investigative Experience: A Sample Form Learner Level

During a major research project, have learners track their progress and sketch the information literacy model they used to accomplish their research. Create a form for your own learners.

My Research Log

My name: _____ Assignment title: _____
(Make a list/log of what you did first, next, next, etc. Include comments about problems you had.)

Self-Assessment Rubric
(Am I an organized investigator? And, Am I making improvement?)

___ My Score

A Drawing of the Information Literacy Model I Used:

The class used this model:

Loertscher's Information Literacy Model

Information Literacy Assessment
Learner Level

Teaching information literacy is a joint responsibility of teacher and library media specialist and is rarely done except as it applys to an information skill to meet a state standard. Here is a cumulative record of a learner's progress over time:

CARMEL CLAY SCHOOLS
Literacy Standards Student Learning Checklist (pilot; excerpt)
Grade 5

Student_____ **Teacher** _____

Exemplary—A student who is performing at an exemplary level is highly motivated and engaged and his/her independent work exceeds grade level expectations.

Proficient—A student who is performing at a proficient level demonstrates consistency in understanding and/or application of grade level standards.

Developing—A student who is performing at a developing level demonstrates inconsistency in understanding and/or application of grade level standards.

Beginning—A student who is performing at a beginning level does not yet appear to understand and/or apply grade level standards.

Standard 8 Information Literacy	October	January	May
Concepts about Media [observations, checklists, individual research log]			
♦ Chose appropriate print, media, and electronic materials to find information.	.		.
♦ Use navigational tools such as electronic card catalog, Internet browsers, and hypermedia.			
Reading [personal reading log, observations, checklists, Accelerated Reader and Reading Counts]			
♦ Read books for enjoyment and information.			
♦ Check out books from the media center on a regular basis.			
♦ Use a dictionary and a thesaurus.			
Information [reference checklist, rubrics]			
♦ Choose/recommend favorite books and authors.			
♦ Find information by using a variety of resources such as, encyclopedias, district web pages, local libraries, community resources, local experts, and interviews.			
♦ Check for information from at least two sources.			
♦ Evaluate search strategy and adopt useful parts of strategy.			
♦ Correctly cite source(s) of information.			

Note: See the balance of the entire instrument on the web site at: http://www.indianalearns.org

Index